SACRAMENTAL GUIDELINES

A Companion to the New Catechism for Religious Educators

KENAN B. OSBORNE, O.F.M.

PAULIST PRESS
New York/Mahwah, N.J.

Special thanks is owed the Religious Education Department of the Diocese of Oakland for reading the manuscript of this work and offering many welcome suggestions for a clearer text.

Cover design by Jim Brisson.

Copyright © 1995 by the Franciscan Friars of California

Library of Congress Cataloging-in-Publication Data

Osborne, Kenan B.
    Sacramental guidelines: a companion to the new catechism for religious educators/Kenan B. Osborne.
      p. cm.
    Includes bibliographical references.
    ISBN 0-8091-3565-5
    1. Sacraments—Catholic Church. 2. Catholic Church—Doctrines.
3. Catholic Church—Liturgy. 4. Catholic Church. Catechismus
Ecclesiae Catholicae. I. Title.
BX2200.O76 1995
264'.0208—dc20   95-3249
                                             CIP

Published by Paulist Press
997 Macarthur Boulevard
Mahwah, New Jersey 07430

Printed and bound in the
United States of America

Contents

1

The Hierarchy of Catholic Truths

One of the paragraphs in the documents from Vatican II which has received considerable attention by both theologians and the hierarchical magisterium of the Roman Catholic Church is found in the *Decree on Ecumenism,* which deals with the "hierarchy of truths of Catholic doctrine."

In comparing doctrines, they should remember that there exists an order or a "hierarchy" of truths in Catholic doctrine, since their relationship to the fundamentals of Christian faith is diverse [11].

The most recent directory for ecumenism, issued in 1993 by the Pontifical Council for Promoting Christian unity, has repeated this same theme of doctrinal hierarchy:

Moreover, the "hierarchy of truths" of Catholic doctrine should always be respected; these truths all demand due assent of faith, yet are not all equally central to the mystery revealed in Jesus Christ, since they vary in their connection with the foundation of the Christian faith [75].

In the arena of religious education the teaching on the "hierarchy of truths" needs to be connected with a second issue, namely, the professional expertise of the religious education teacher. In the NCCB document *Basic Teachings for Catholic Religious Education* [1973], the bishops of the United States expressed a desire that there be an informed laity, people of faith, who know their religion and can give an account of it [pp.

2–3]. These same words were repeated in their *Guidelines for Doctrinally Sound Catechetical Materials* [1990, p. 9] and in this document the bishops cited this statement as the very goal or reason for writing the new guidelines.

Religious education teachers are central to this goal of developing an informed laity, since much of the basic education in our faith rests on their work. However, religious education teachers can only do this if they themselves are quite aware of the hierarchy of truths, and in their religious education classes present the material in an ordered and hierarchically structured way. In other words, religious education teachers must have not only some general awareness of the "hierarchy of truths," but they must also be able to distinguish in adequate detail the order of truths within this hierarchy. Only then will they be able to present the truths of our faith in this hierarchical way.

This small volume is meant to help religious education teachers do precisely this as regards the sacraments. By no means does this present volume intend to present a full picture of the Christian sacraments; other books will remain necessary for such a full catechetical presentation. The new catechism is surely one of these books, and this volume is meant to move along the same structured format of the catechism, and indicate step-by-step and in a clear pedagogical way the hierarchy of truths involved in sacramental instruction. My aim is, therefore, quite modest: namely, to provide religious education teachers, on the issue of our Christian sacraments, with a clear indication of the following three general or major categories in the hierarchy of truths:

1. The teachings on the sacraments which are foundational to Catholic faith, that is, the solemn, official teachings of the church. These are often called the immutable teachings of the church and must be presented in that way to students.

2. The teachings on the sacraments which are currently official teaching of the church, but which in the course of time may change. These are official church teachings, but at the same time they are not immutable. These teachings must be presented in that way to students.

3. The teachings on the sacraments which reputable Catholic theologians teach, but which are at this point in time merely theological views. These theological views are acceptable Catholic views,

but since theologians often differ, these teachings are areas on sacramental theology which remain unresolved, and they must be presented in that way to students.

These are the three major categories, which make up this "hierarchy of truths of Catholic doctrine." Theologians have often made further distinctions within each of these three major categories, but each and every one of our church's specific teachings can be classified under one of these headings. Let us consider these three major categories more carefully.

1. THE FIRST CATEGORY IN THE HIERARCHY OF DOCTRINES:

Official and Solemn Teachings of the Church.

Teachings of the Roman Catholic Church, which are the most official and solemn, are those religious teachings that:

a. have been clearly and solemnly defined either by church councils or by a pope; or
b. are contained in the sacred scriptures in such a way that Christian tradition has *consistently* held them to be true.

When teachings have been defined by church councils or by a pope, they are called teachings of the *extraordinary magisterium* of the church.

2. THE SECOND CATEGORY IN THE HIERARCHY OF DOCTRINES:

Undefined but Official Teachings of Church Leadership.

Secondly, there are church teachings, which at a given time in history are the official positions of the current church leadership. These are positions which are not solemnly defined in any way; have not been consistently held by church tradition; but are, nonetheless, official teachings of the church at a given time. For sacramental theology and its liturgy, one finds, today, this kind of teaching primarily in three official sets of church documents:

a. In the documents of Vatican II, through which the bishops deliberately did not intend to define any doctrine, but did intend to present officially a way of teaching and celebrating the sacraments for our time.

b. In the various revised sacramental rituals which were authorized by the bishops at the Second Vatican Council, and which were drawn up and officially promulgated after Vatican II.

c. In the revised code of canon law promulgated in 1983.

There are, as well, a few, smaller publications on specific sacramental issues, which from time to time have been issued either by the Vatican or by national conferences of bishops or by individual bishops, and which contain official directives on the sacraments. All of these documents—the conciliar documents, the sacramental rituals, the code of canon law and the other selected official directives—are called teachings of the *ordinary magisterium* of the church.

3. THE THIRD CATEGORY IN THE HIERARCHY OF DOCTRINES:

Acceptable Theological Opinions.

Thirdly—and this group of teachings comprises the largest category of the sacramental teaching—there are the various theological ways in which the Roman Catholic faith has been presented in a systematic way by theologians. These positions of various theologians are neither defined teachings of the church, nor are they presented as official teachings by ordinary hierarchical magisterium. These theological positions are the views of various theologians. In the history of Christian theology, there have even been schools of various theological views, such as the Dominican or Thomistic school of theology, the Franciscan or Scotistic school of theology, and the Augustinian school of theology, to name only three of the more prominent "schools." All of these various theological views are basically opinions, and, in a hierarchy of doctrines, they have neither more nor less validity than the coherent strength or incoherent weakness of the views which they represent. As such, they should not and cannot be presented in religious education classes as the "official teaching" of the church. Nor should church leadership ever present them as official teachings of the church.

The fundamental pedagogical reason why this hierarchy of truths is necessary for religious education is this: a religious education teacher, using as background a textbook such as the new catechism or a book on sacramental theology, should be able to distinguish very clearly, with the help of such reference books, these three categories of church teaching and, consequently, be able to convey to the students this hierarchy of truths. If this is not done, students too easily come to the conclusion that everything they learn in a religion class is "church doctrine." When changes take place, such people too often think that the very "teaching of the church" is being changed, and because of this misconception, their faith seems to be challenged at its very roots. We have seen instances of this in the aftermath of Vatican II, since many people had been taught in and through catechisms and other textbooks that everything in such books was the teaching of the church. Today's religious education programs must avoid repeating this kind of religious education and must take seriously the call by Vatican II to specify in as clear a way as possible the hierarchy of Catholic truths.

To provide a better indication of this hierarchy of truths, an example might be helpful. Even though later on in this volume, we will consider the sundry issues involved in the sacrament of confirmation, I would like to use the theology of this sacrament of confirmation as a preliminary exemplification of the necessity and the value for making distinctions based on the hierarchy of Catholic truths. As all religious educators know, preparing young people for confirmation and preparing parents for their children's confirmation is not an easy task. As we shall see, one of the major reasons for this uneasiness is the lack of a clear theology on confirmation, even though there are immutable truths involved and even though there are official but mutable truths involved.

1. DEFINED, OFFICIAL, AND SOLEMN TEACHINGS

The defined, official and solemn teachings of the church are issues which every religious education teacher *must include* in any course, since these are the "dogmas" or the "unchangeable teachings" or the "solemn doctrine" of the Roman Catholic Church.[1] Students in a Catholic religious education classroom should understand that these teachings are not simply opinions or temporary regulations. Rather, they represent a very solemn, often defined, and therefore profoundly official stance of the entire Roman Catholic community. Christians respond to the reality behind these official and solemn teachings through an act of faith.

---

[1] The precise term for this kind of immutable teaching varies: some authors will use the term, "dogma"; others will use "church doctrine" or "defined teaching." The name is not the issue here; the issue is that corpus of teaching by the church which forms an unchangeable core.

As regards the sacrament of confirmation, there have been three solemnly defined statements:

1. The first is that confirmation is a sacrament;
2. The second is that the sacrament of confirmation confers a sacramental character.
3. The third is that a bishop is the ordinary minister of confirmation.

If all that religious educators had to do was teach the young people these three ideas, preparation for the sacrament of confirmation would be an easy task. However, it is clear that these three issues do not really express all that Catholics understand about the sacrament of confirmation. Issues are defined, generally, when there is a major controversy, and it was precisely because of certain controversies that these three issues were defined in a special way at the Council of Trent. There were certain Protestant teachers who denied that confirmation was a sacrament. They found no clear basis for a sacrament of confirmation in the New Testament, and so the claim was made that bishops in some former time had made up this sacrament and imposed it on the church. The bishops at the Council of Trent rejected this view and solemnly defined confirmation to be one of the seven sacraments of the church.

Today, we realize that confirmation developed out of the baptismal ritual, and in the early church the rites of anointing and laying on of hands, which we, today, call confirmation, were simply an integral part of the baptismal sacrament itself. In the course of time, but only in the Western church, a separation did take place, but confirmation always retained a connection to baptism. It is because of this original relationship to the sacrament of baptism that one can say: confirmation is a sacrament. If this relationship of confirmation to baptismal theology were ever removed, one would find it very difficult to maintain the defined doctrine on the sacramentality of confirmation.

Because of this original relationship of confirmation to baptism, one can also speak of the sacramental character of confirmation. Baptism confers a character, and this belief was part of the thinking of the early church. When confirmation began to be separated from baptism, bishops and theologians maintained that confirmation also conferred a character. Again, however, they were able to teach this because of confirmation's original relationship to baptism.

In the Western church, the bishop was the ordinary minister of confirmation. In the Eastern churches, baptism continued to include the rites of anointing and laying on of hands—rituals that the West uses for confirmation—and since in the Eastern churches the minister of baptism was a priest, and not necessarily a bishop, the issue of an "ordinary" minister for confirmation never arose for these Eastern churches. In the West, the ministerial role of the bishop was emphasized for a very sound reason: namely, a person is not baptized or confirmed in a small local church—a village or parish church. The true meaning of "local church" was a diocese and the presence of the bishop indicated a belonging to a larger local church, a diocese, as well as to a universal church.

Even though today we know far more about the history of this sacrament of confirmation, and how it developed from the sacrament of baptism, there is still something very special about confirmation: it is a sacrament, which means that we celebrate in confirmation the very action of God in a person's life and not merely some human action. Moreover, we celebrate an action of God which God will never annul, and this is precisely the point behind the teaching that confirmation confers a character. Finally, our baptism/confirmation is an initiation into the mystery of the church: into a local church, a diocese, and into the church catholic. The presence of a bishop indicates the largeness of this church to which we belong.

There are other defined doctrines which affect confirmation, namely, those defined doctrines which are common to all the ritualized sacraments. These, too, could be added to this section of a preparation for confirmation, but even then, as every teacher can see, a mere presentation of the defined dogmas would not truly present the height and depth, length and breadth of this holy sacrament.

However, the teaching of these dogmas or doctrines cannot simply involve the communication of a propositional statement. At the core of each of these teachings there is a truth of faith which is intended to nourish one's spiritual life. Dogmas are not, therefore, simply matters of intellectual assent. As *truths of faith,* they nourish and strengthen one's faith and one's spirituality. Every good catechism or book on the sacraments, which presents these dogmas or truths, would do well to indicate, as clearly as possible, the major ways through which these same dogmas or truths foster the growth of one's spirituality. In religious education, dogma and spirituality cannot be divorced from each other. In the chapters which follow, I will indicate at each step some ideas on a relationship between a specific, defined teaching and Christian spirituality, and hopefully these observations will assist the religious education teacher in his or her work.

There is yet another issue which the hierarchy of truths indicates: namely, even within the church teachings which are the official, solemn dogma or doctrine of the faith, some of these teachings are of greater importance than others. In other words, there is a "hierarchy of defined or solemn truths." That there is a God is, surely, the most fundamental of all these truths. That God became human in Jesus is certainly a most fundamental truth. All other dogmas or defined teachings presuppose and depend on this fundamental Christian belief. Were one to attempt a list of this hierarchy of solemn truths or dogmas, no total agreement would prevail. Nonetheless, this kind of hierarchy was clearly meant by the bishops at Vatican II when they approved the statement in *Gaudium et Spes,* and this kind of hierarchy is also indicated in the 1993 *Directory for Ecumenism.*

2. OFFICIAL TEACHINGS OF THE ORDINARY MAGISTERIUM OF THE CHURCH

The second group of doctrines are called the "ordinary magisterium of the church," as distinguished from the "extraordinary magisterium of the church." Extraordinary magisterium has been exercised in two papal infallible statements on the Blessed Virgin Mary, and in various doctrines infallibly defined by church councils. This second level in the hierarchy of truths, the ordinary magisterium, represents a lesser grade of official teaching.[2] Nonetheless, such teachings are official teachings presented by church authority for the current and proper order of church life. In religious education, students should be taught that these teachings are official, even though they are not immutable. In their studies, for instance, students will discover that sacramental rituals during the course of history have changed dramatically. They will also find out that canon law has in the course of history often been changed. If some teaching has from time to time been changed, religious education students will invariably ask: "Why do we have to accept them now? Why do we have to obey them now?"

To answer such questions, a religious education teacher can neither present this kind of church teaching as unchangeable teachings of the

---

[2] Prior to Vatican II the term, "ordinary magisterium," was used by theologians for bishops who taught a doctrine even though they were not gathered into a council. Extraordinary magisterium was used when bishops gathered together in a council and made conciliar statements. Vatican II, however, has altered this way of speaking, since the bishops were gathered in a conciliar situation but the bishops made no "definitions" of any doctrine. I realize that other theologians may describe "ordinary magisterium" in a way different than the way that I use it in the text. However, because of the Vatican II situation, a commonly acceptable description of "ordinary magisterium" remains in the air. I do not want to appear defensive of my own use of this term, since the term is secondary. What I am concerned about in this section of the text is basically those official teachings which can be changed. It is this idea which distinguishes the material of this section of the text from that of the "defined teaching" and from that of "theological opinion."

church, nor can he or she present them as infallible doctrines. Whenever, in the past, religious education teachers and theologians have attempted to present such teachings as the teachings of the church, which almost implies that such teachings are immutable, many students at some later period in their lives have discovered that this kind of presentation was not the case and, in many instances, these students, now quite grown up, have become confused and even disillusioned. Religious education teachers, as well as professional theologians, must be honest and above-board on this issue of what is changeable and what is not changeable in the church. If they do not do this, an injustice is done both to the student and to the church itself. Indeed, the religious education program itself suffers whenever teachers do not make necessary distinctions on the matter of church doctrine.

In the example of confirmation, where do we find these official but changeable teachings? First of all, the revised rituals for the sacrament of confirmation should be carefully studied. These rituals are official, and a celebration of confirmation is meant to follow the prescriptions of the rituals. Currently, one will find a ritual for confirmation in the *RCIA;* another is found in the more recent publication of the rite of baptism for children of catechetical age; a third ritual is the revised rite of confirmation itself. In these rituals, one finds beautiful prayers that speak about the meaning of confirmation. One finds along with these prayers a ritual of anointing and a ritual of laying on of hands, rituals which have a rich and powerful religious history. Religious education teachers can draw countless images from these prayers and actions, and use such images to indicate what the church is celebrating in a ritual of confirmation.

To a lesser degree, the revised code of canon law can also be used to discover official but changeable truths regarding the sacrament of confirmation. The regulations which are found in this volume of church laws are certainly official and should be followed, but just as in our lifetime we have seen a revision of canon law, so perhaps in the lifetime of our students there could be another revision. Such revisions indicate very clearly that these official teachings are mutable.

Students, of course, will invariably ask: "Why do we have to obey these regulations if they can be changed?" There is no simple answer to this kind of question. Perhaps one could provide some answer by describing the context which one finds in any genuine leadership situation, whether in the family, in civil government, or in the church. Church leadership at a given period of time—in ways similar to any other leadership group—has both the right and the obligation to establish official regulations, e.g., an official ritual for the celebration of each of the sacraments. In doing this, church leadership, acting precisely in its leadership role, makes sure that the manner in which the celebrations of baptism, eucharist, reconciliation, or any other sacrament will truly represent in its ritualization the sacramental mystery which it is meant to celebrate. Such regulations are not presented as merely "suggestions for worship," for there is something mandatory about them, and because they are presented as mandatory by the "ordinary magisterium" of the church, they are official. However, since such rituals can change and will be changed in the future, just as they have been changed in the past, they cannot be presented in a course on religious education as unchangeable. We are asked to accept them because of obedience to rightful leadership.

A contemporary, highly-publicized example might clarify this. In the church today, the official ritual for celebrating the eucharist is the new post-Vatican II ritual. According to this ritual, the eucharist can be celebrated in every vernacular language. There is even an official Latin form of this revised ritual, which is found in the missal itself and which can be licitly used. This new eucharistic ritual is, in many ways, different from the so-called "tridentine mass." The tridentine mass stems from a ritual which was promulgated after the Council of Trent and which remained a standard part of the Roman Catholic Church from the sixteenth century down to the post-Vatican II period, when it was officially changed. The tridentine mass was celebrated only in Latin. The priest, and he alone (with but a few exceptions, such as the *Kyrie*, the *Amens*, the *Sanctus*, and a few other prayers), prayed the entire mass by himself, with his back to the people. Because almost every ritualized act in the tridentine mass was rigidly established, the celebration of mass was the same all over the world, no matter where one was. The identical Latin celebration of mass took place in every country. Roman Catholics who travelled could attend the tridentine mass and understand what was going on. Today, the tridentine form of the mass remains a *valid* way of celebrating the eucharist, but it is not the officially authorized way of celebrating the eucharist today. As a result, the celebration of the tridentine mass today *would be valid but illicit,* unless special permission by church leadership has been given to a certain group of Roman Catholics to celebrate the eucharist according to this former ritual. In actual fact, there are a few Roman Catholic groups who have requested and received special permission to continue celebrating the tridentine mass on specific occasions. There are, however, other Roman Catholics, priests and lay people, who without any proper authorization by church authority continue to celebrate the tridentine mass. These Roman Catholics, more often than not, openly defy church authority on this matter, and at times they even state that the new Vatican II ritual for the mass is "wrong," is a "disgrace," or even is "heretical." This latter group of people, who on the one hand attest to their loyalty as Roman Catholics, are actually defying the ordinary magisterium of the Roman Catholic Church in their refusal to acknowledge the new eucharistic rituals.

In this example, we see several issues:

1. Many Roman Catholics struggle in their conscience to distinguish the changeable from the unchangeable as regards the various teachings of the Roman Catholic Church. One of the major reasons why these Catholics endure such a struggle is that these people were, in their youth, never taught how to distinguish the changeable from the unchangeable. They were taught that the mass, i.e., the tridentine mass, was unchangeable. They may have been taught by well-meaning teachers, but what they were taught on this issue was incorrect. They have continued to believe, however, that what they were taught was correct. Some even go so far as to hang on to "what they were taught" even though the ordinary magisterium of the church today is teaching something different. The lesson, which those in religious education must see in this situation, is the need at every level of religious education to make sure, as best one can, that the hierarchy of teachings be clearly presented.

2. Secondly, religious education teachers will see in the example above that there is a legitimate role for Roman Catholic leadership and in issues of ordinary magisterium, Roman Catholics are required to obey. Naturally, this kind of obedience is not the same as one's obedience to official, solemn or defined teachings of the church, but it is in its own way a required form of obedience. However, there is also a correlative responsibility of church leadership, which can never present these kinds of teachings as though they were "infallible" or absolutely true. Church leadership itself, in order to be credible and responsible, must distinguish the hierarchy of teachings and make this hierarchy of truths clear in its own presentation of church doctrine.

3. It is evident to religious education teachers that, in the example of the tridentine mass, the focal issue eventually was changed. At first, the focal issue was the correct ritual for the eucharistic celebration. In the course of the debate, however, the focal issue became "church authority." This kind of shift has happened time and time again. A sacramental issue or a moral issue begins as something specifically sacramental or moral, but in the course of the debate the focal issue becomes an issue of church authority. In the area of sacraments, such matters as the tridentine mass, the requirement of first confession prior to first eucharist, the issue of altar girls, have changed their central focus. The persistent questioning of these issues has come to be seen as a questioning of church authority.

The teaching on a hierarchy of truths involves yet another set of distinctions: namely, within the official church teachings, which though solemn are still changeable, there is a hierarchy of values. Some of these teachings are more important than others. Certain encyclicals are more important than other encyclicals; certain statements from a Vatican congregation are more important than other statements, even issued by the same Vatican congregation. However, it is very difficult at times to assess this ranking of value. In the procedures of the Vatican there exists a wide variety of forms which one might use to issue a solemn but changeable teaching: for example, documents are called by a variety of names: "an instruction," "guidelines," "letter." The pope himself uses a variety of terms for his own statements. Each of these has some more or less level of rank, which can be easily overlooked. Today's media, in a particular way, overlooks any nuance of this hierarchy, and newspapers and television are filled with the "latest" authoritative statement from the Vatican. Even though there is some confusion in all of this, the hierarchy of truths does intend to differentiate those truths of the solemn, official, but changeable teachings of the church into some sort of ranking.

3. ACCEPTABLE THEOLOGICAL OPINIONS

Theologians have a major role in the formation of church teaching. In 1989 the bishops of the United States issued a statement called *Doctrinal Responsibilities.* The goal of this document was meant to promote the cooperation between bishops and theologians. In this document one finds a description of the theologian's task [p. 5]:

A theologian is one "who seeks to mediate, through the discipline of scholarship, between living faith and the culture it is called to transform."

"Grounded in the commitment of their ecclesial faith and trained in the skills of scholarship, theologians systematically explore the nature and foundations of God's revelation and the teaching of the church."

"The contribution and cogency of a theologian's work, therefore, depend upon scholarly competence that is rooted in faith and is faithful to the church's teaching under the guidance of the Holy Spirit. That competence can be assessed from the quality of the evidence theologians adduce and the soundness of the arguments they advance for the sake of Christ's truth."

Theologians draw together in as unified a way as possible the various solemn, official unchanging truths of our faith, as well as the solemn, official changing truths of our faith. To do this, they bring to these issues a large variety of material. Some of this material is taken from the fathers of the church and major theologians of the past; some is taken from a clearer insight into history, especially the history of the church, the history of biblical material, and the history of doctrines; some is taken from other sciences, such as philosophy, sociology, cultural anthropology, psychology.

As one reads this guide, it will be increasingly evident that the defined doctrines of the church on sacraments represent, at best, only a very small percentage of the material called "sacramental theology." This indicates that very little sacramental theology has ever been officially and solemnly defined by the church. Very little sacramental theology, therefore, is unchangeable. This does not infer that this "very little" is of no consequence. Rather, the opposite is true: this "very little," though small, is very important and highly significant for understanding sacraments.

The teachings of the ordinary magisterium on sacraments, as found in rituals and codes, are somewhat more extensive. This kind of sacramental teaching would, if compressed together, make up perhaps a third of the material found in a book on sacramental theology. This material of the ordinary magisterium centers primarily around the way in which today's church leadership has authorized the celebration of the individual sacraments. In earlier periods of church history, the ritualized celebration of the sacraments took place in different and quite varied ways, as the history of theology and liturgy indicates. In the future, the present Vatican II rituals will surely be changed again. Neither the contemporary sacramental rituals with their precise regulations for liturgical celebrations nor the revised code of canon law in its section on sacraments can be presented to students in a religious education class as unchangeable teachings of the church.

Given all of the above, one will clearly perceive that the majority of the material on the sacraments must be regarded as simply theological explanations, not church doctrine. Theological explanations or opinions are a necessary part of sacramental catechesis, since the role of theology is to help unify the few and disparate defined teachings of the church. Theological explanations take into consideration both the extraordinary teachings of the magisterium and also the ordinary teachings of the magisterium (e.g., sacramental rituals and sections of the code of canon law on the sacraments). Inasmuch as it is possible, theology attempts to bring this disparate material into some sort of unified presentation. Theology does this by filling in the areas of non-relationship with some sort of solid theological presentation.

The greatest Christian theologians have always tried to unify the various parts of our Christian faith. At the beginning of the third century in Alexandria, Egypt, Origen, a major theologian of the early church, wrote one of the first unified "theological" treatises, called "First Principles." Centuries later, in the medieval period, many theologians produced books called a *Summa*. The *Summa theologiae* of St. Thomas Aquinas is probably the best known. In the period from the Council of Trent down to Vatican II, many Catholic writers published "manuals of theology" which again were attempts to unify various religious themes. During the nineteenth and twentieth centuries, these manuals were used in the seminaries. Roman Catholic theologians have consistently attempted to unify the few and somewhat disparate key pieces of official doctrine, both defined and undefined, into an intelligible whole, a *Summa*.

All these theologians also realized that their attempts at unity had a disunified side as well. Thomas Aquinas found that not every aspect of church doctrine and theology could be logically integrated into a "system." As a consequence, Thomas created his "theological unity," his *Summa,* by placing those themes and ideas, which defied any logical integration, in one place rather than another on the basis of *convenientia;* that is, in his view, these parts of the theological picture *seemed to fit better,* i.e., more conveniently, in one place rather than in another. Moreover, in a quite gentle way, Thomas Aquinas continually made mention of theologically competing but nonetheless legitimate views, developed by other theologians. This acknowledgement of competing but legitimate views was another indication that there was a certain disunity within a unity. As a result, this kind of theological book has been called a *Summa,* not a synthesis. A *Summa* is a gathering together of theological and doctrinal material in as unified a way as possible, but not in any totally organic or systematic way.

In n. 11 of the *Catechism of the Catholic Church* the idea of a unity is expressed:

> This catechism aims at presenting an organic synthesis of the foundations and essential content of Catholic doctrine, as regards both faith and morals, in the light of the Second Vatican Council and the whole of the Church's Tradition.

Such an aim, of necessity, involves theological views or opinions. The few, occasional solemn definitions of the church, and the somewhat more extensive teachings of the ordinary magisterium, when taken by themselves, can never form an organic synthesis. Theological opinions have consistently been the material which brings such teachings into a unified framework, along the lines of a *Summa.*

Let us return to the example of confirmation. There is a theological issue regarding confirmation, which as of right now has not been settled. Theologians and bishops present various views. The issue concerns the proper age for confirmation. This unresolved issue about age governs almost all discussion on the sacrament of confirmation, and once a particular age is determined for a given diocese, then the theology of confirmation used by religious education teachers in that same diocese is also colored by the age selected. In one diocese, the bishop might determine that the age for confirmation in his diocese will be the final year of high school. In another diocese, which could be a neighboring diocese, a different bishop might determine that fourth grade is the proper age. The way in which religious education teachers will present the sacrament of confirmation to seniors in high school will not be the same as the way other religious education teachers will present the sacrament of confirmation to fourth graders.

The recent decision of the National Conference of Catholic Bishops on the age of confirmation [1994] indicates that the proper age for confirmation in the United States is between seven and seventeen. This decision, approved by the Holy See, indicates a span of ten years within which confirmation is licitly administered for those baptized as infants or as children. Nonetheless, the pedagogical differences between a seven-year-old and a seventeen-year-old are profound. Religious education teachers will shape their confirmation presentations differently, depending on the age-level.

There are good theological, pastoral and liturgical reasons for an early age of confirmation as well as good theological, pastoral and liturgical reasons for a later age of confirmation. What one confronts here is an unresolved theological issue. However, even though it is only a theological issue, not a defined doctrine; even though it is unresolved and disputed by theologians and determined differently by various bishops, this issue of age colors almost everything involved in the religious educator's preparation for confirmation, both the preparation of the young people to be confirmed, as also the preparation of the parents of these young people.

In all of the sacraments it is important for a religious education teacher to be aware of the unresolved issues. The new catechism, in its treatment of the sacraments, tends to pass over in silence almost all the disputed areas, even though—as we see above in the age issue of confirmation—these unresolved theological issues can, and most often do, affect one's whole sacramental presentation.

In the subsequent pages on the various sacraments, I will use the following structure to clarify the hierarchy of truths:

1. First of all, I will present a brief statement which expresses the official church teaching.

2. Second, I will indicate the main official documentation for this solemn teaching of the church.

3. Third, I will add some comments which are meant to provide a religious education teacher with key background material as regards each of the solemn official teachings of the church.

4. Fourth, I will present the major themes of the changeable positions of the church vis-à-vis the sacraments.

5. Fifth, I will present a list of pertinent issues in sacramental theology which are still unresolved.

Moreover, since these doctrines are not simply intellectual issues, the final comments in each section of stage three will offer some suggestions on ways to relate the "defined teaching" to our Christian spirituality. This final comment will begin with the title: Relationship to Christian spirituality. Hopefully, the connections of official church doctrine to the area of spirituality will provide some sort of assistance to religious education teachers who try so hard to make the faith of their students not merely an intellectual procedure, but a living and spiritual reality.

Finally, there is an issue which I do not even begin to address in this present book. It is the issue of culture. In the area of liturgy and sacraments, cultural issues are usually presented from an Anglo-American/European standpoint. The underlying philosophy and worldview in most of the sacramental rites, canons and theology have been presented from a clearly Anglo-American/European worldview. The theological vocabulary in this body of material is Anglo-American/European. The theology is Anglo-American/European. These works are primarily "first world," not "third world" volumes. Even though sacramental studies attempt to describe a "universal" position, their very construction is not universal.

Their terminology and their underlying philosophical ethos are not universal. The way in which they present sacramental theology is not universal. Mere translation of these volumes into a different language outside the culture in which they were written does not change much. Inculturation and acculturation are much more than mere translation.

In our North American classrooms today, we do not have only Anglo-American/European students. We have students from a rich variety of Hispanic, Asian, African, Native American cultures, as well as from other very distinct and important cultures. We teach in a multicultural framework. An increasing majority of our religious education students have neither the worldview nor the philosophical background of an Anglo-American/European. I have no solution to this problem, and I make no attempt to offer one. However, as every religious education teacher in North America knows already, the issue of multiculturalism is not a peripheral issue to sound pedagogy. It is today a central and major issue. Inculturation and acculturation are not achieved simply by the use of a vernacular; nor are they achieved simply by the use of local songs or local art work. Such elements are necessary for inculturation and acculturation, but there is much more involved, namely a total rethinking and reexperiencing of a reality, presented basically in an Anglo-American/European context in and through the very thought processes and experiencing processes of a given non-Anglo-American/European culture.

Stop

Before you turn another page, remember you are entering the area of sacramental theology with major presuppositions.

PRESUPPOSITIONS ABOUT
GOD
JESUS
CHURCH
RELIGION
THE MEANING OF LIFE

Before you turn the page, remember you are entering the area of sacramental theology with a complex personal background of human experience.

HUMAN EXPERIENCE ABOUT
RELATIONSHIPS
SELF-IDENTITY
SELF-IMAGE
SELF-DETERMINATION
THE MEANING OF
MALE/FEMALE

Your students also bring their presuppositions (which may not be exactly yours) and their human experience (which is certainly not yours) into the study of sacramental theology. All of this, your own and your students', will be part of the way in which you understand, present, and spiritualize sacramental theology. There will be times when an issue arises that causes serious difficulty. This issue might be triggered by some aspect regarding confirmation, by an aspect regarding eucharist, by an aspect regarding reconciliation, etc. The difficulty, however, is actually not a sacramental one, but rather one which involves one's presuppositions of life experience. Whenever this occurs, a major pedagogical help is the following:

> Remember that quite possibly, the difficulty may not lie in confirmation, eucharist, reconciliation, etc., but rather in the area of one's presuppositions or in the area of one's life experience.

> When this happens, back away from the sacramental issue under consideration and begin to unpack with your students the presuppositions which are involved and the life experiences which are also involved.

With this caveat on presuppositions and life experience as a part of your journey into sacramental theology, please turn the page.

2

The Sacramental Dispensation

The way in which the *Catechism of the Catholic Church* begins its presentation on sacraments is an excellent pedagogical model for religious educators. The authors begin their sacramental theology with a far-reaching overview on the very notion of liturgy in the life of a Christian community. To provide for this broad liturgical context of the sacramental reality, the authors deal first with the sacramental dispensation, or more specifically, the paschal mystery in the life of the church; and then with the nature and essential features of liturgical celebration, the paschal mystery in the church's sacramental life.

In courses on the sacraments, religious educators could easily mirror this kind of approach, with a prefatory unit on the issue of liturgical and symbolic celebration, including non-Christian liturgies and symbols, as well as Christian ones. After this first unit, the religious education teacher could move to a second unit on the ritualized sacraments.

The overarching and most fundamental theme, which the *Catechism of the Catholic Church* develops as regards all liturgical celebrations of the Catholic Church, is clearly stated:

> What the church's liturgy primarily celebrates is the paschal mystery by which Christ saved us [1067].

On the basis of this general statement the catechism proceeds to underline four basic ideas, which undergird all liturgical and sacramental life. These four ideas constitute, for a religious education teacher, a solid framework not only for an overarching framework of liturgical, sacramental life taken in a general way, but for each of the particular sacraments as well.

1. The primacy of God's action. Liturgy centers on the spiritual blessings which God gives us [1083] and only on this prior basis does liturgy become a community's response of faith and love. Such an emphasis is basic for all catechesis on the sacraments: namely, Christian liturgy is primarily a celebration of God's action, and only secondarily a response of the church, an action of the people of God. On occasion, religious educators have spent more time on the "response" side: namely, on what the church community does—its songs, its readings, its prayers, etc.—rather than on the celebration of God's love. Religious educators should continually stress the action of God in sacramental catechesis. God's action is the primary basis for all liturgical and sacramental celebration, and the community's liturgical action is a secondary response to the action of God.

2. The centrality of Christ. Liturgy primarily celebrates the paschal mystery by which Christ saved us [1067]. It is Christ's own prayer in which we share [1073]; it is Christ's mystery [1075]; it is Christ living and acting within his church [1076]; it is Christ signifying and making present his paschal mystery [1085]; it is Christ being present in all the sacraments [1088]. These are but some of the major statements about the centrality of the action and real presence of Christ in all liturgy, but especially in the sacramental liturgy.

3. The Spirit of Jesus. The Holy Spirit is also central to liturgy, but the catechism continually stresses the relationship of the Holy Spirit to Jesus. The Holy Spirit prepares us for Christ [1093 ff.; 1099 ff.; 1104 ff.]. The Holy Spirit is sent to us in every liturgical action to bring us into communion with Christ. Once again, the emphasis on the centrality of Christ is clearly evident, even in its presentation of the Holy Spirit. The Holy Spirit and Christ cannot be separated in sacramental life.

4. The community called church. The term, "church," when used in sacramental theology, generally means the community of believers, not church leadership or the ordained presiders. In the documents of Vatican II, the church itself is presented as a basic sacrament. The sacraments are dispensed by the church, for the church itself is the sacrament of Christ's action, at work through the mission of the Holy Spirit.

That the church itself is a basic sacrament can be found in *Lumen Gentium,* art. 1, 9, 48; *Gaudium et Spes,* 45; *Sacrosanctum Concilium,* 2, 5, 26; *Ad Gentes,* 5. The major commentaries on the documents of Vatican II (G. Philips, B. Kloppenburg, H. Vorgrimler) state clearly that the bishops at Vatican II stressed two major themes on church:

1. the church as the people of God;
2. the church as a sacrament.

This teaching is clearly a teaching of the ordinary magisterium of the church and cannot be minimized or left to one side. Religious education teachers have frequently heard from the hierarchical magisterium that the church is indeed a basic sacrament. Whenever contemporary books on the sacraments pass over this teaching of the magisterium in their discussion of the sacraments, religious educators cannot help but be somewhat bewildered. They ask how can such a teaching, which is ordinary magisterium, not be an integral part of sacramental teaching?

A few words of clarification on this issue of the church as a basic sacrament might be of help to a religious education teacher. Some theologians have attempted to clarify the meaning of the church as a "basic sacrament," by saying that the use of the term, "sacrament," for the church is to be understood in an analogous way. This is not the place to enter into a lengthy discussion of this issue, but whenever one uses the term, "analogous," there must be a primary "analogue." Is the church as a basic sacrament the "primary analogue"? Or are the seven sacraments the "primary analogue"? If the church is the primary analogue for sacramentality, then one must say:

> Because the church itself is a sacrament, therefore the seven rituals are also sacramental.

If, however, the seven sacraments are the primary analogue, then one must say:

> Because the seven rituals are sacraments, the church itself can be called sacramental.

This is not simply a matter of words. Among various sacramental and liturgical traditions, fidelity to apostolic tradition has been a key criterion for judging what is correct and what is not correct. Since holy order is one of the seven sacraments, and since apostolic succession is, in the above statement, connected to the episcopal hierarchy, for the bishops are the successors of the apostles, the two ways of considering the primary analogue play a major theological role. In the first approach, one would say:

> Because the church itself is sacramental, therefore bishops—and they are the successors of the apostles—are sacramental.

The theological criterion or primary analogue in this instance is the basic sacramentality of the church. All sacraments, including holy order, are sacraments only because the church itself is a more basic sacrament.

In the second approach, one would say:

> Because the bishops themselves are sacramental—and they are the successors to the apostles—therefore the church under such bishops is also sacramental.

The theological criterion or primary analogue in this instance is the sacramentality of the episcopal hierarchy. Those who are truly bishops are truly the successors of the apostles and are, therefore, truly the apostolic criterion for all sacramentality, including the sacramentality of the church.

This discussion of the issue of the church as a basic sacrament and of its correlative issue that Jesus, in his humanity, is the primordial sacrament can be found in such major authors as Casel, Rahner, Semmelroth, and Schillebeeckx. These scholars had considerable influence on the way in which the documents of Vatican II were drawn up. Surely, religious educators are aware of this contemporary sacramental approach and emphasis. It is found in almost every book on sacraments they read; it is mentioned again and again in almost every talk on the sacraments which they have heard at various institutes and congresses. It is stated clearly in the documents of Vatican II.

On the one hand, religious educators have heard from the Vatican itself, i.e., in the conciliar documents of Vatican II, strong statements that the church is a basic sacrament. On the other hand, whenever religious educators hear only a whisper about this matter in another official document, we have a classic instance of mixed signals. From one and the same source, one hears two different voices. It is precisely because of the continuance of these kinds of mixed signals—and this is only one of several such cases—that Roman Catholic religious education today experiences some pedagogical confusion. Thousands of religious education teachers have received such mixed signals and they cannot help but ask themselves: "Given these mixed signals, what am I supposed to teach?"

However, more is at stake here than simply a silence on the theme that the church is a basic sacrament and a lack of incorporating this teaching of the sacramentality of the church into a presentation on sacraments. Important as this teaching about the sacramentality of the church is for sacramental theology, an even more fundamental and therefore more disturbing aspect of such silence or lack of incorporation is the following. Whenever a document or book which claims to make a presentation of what is doctrinally common to the Catholic sacraments passes over an issue of church doctrine, such as the teaching that the church is a basic sacrament, promulgated so strongly in conciliar documents, a question of the value of church magisterium itself arises. Because of the emphasis on the church as a sacrament in the documents of Vatican II, this teaching of the church as basic sacrament can only be considered today as part of the ordinary magisterium. The non-incorporation of this approach into one's sacramental theology raises a question: when does one have to follow the ordinary magisterium of the church? Why can the authors of such works appear to disregard a teaching of the ordinary magisterium of the church? There is no good answer to this question.

The following list is intended to provide a basic point of reference for a religious education teacher to distinguish the immutable from the changeable. I have cited some documentation for the "officialness," "solemnity" or "defined status," of the church. Usually, these citations are references to the Council of Trent, particularly the canons on each of the sacraments (abbreviated as can.). However, these references to Trent only mean that in these canons a "solemn and official" teaching of the church appears. One cannot say because it is a canon of Trent, therefore it is defined. The "definition" or "solemn and official" aspect of the teaching derives from many other sources beyond these canons which must also be taken into account. Otherwise, one would have to say that every canon of the Council of Trent represents "defined" doctrine, and this has never been held in the Roman Catholic Church. Accordingly, the references are meant for teachers should they wish documentation for their class preparation.

Sacraments in General
Defined Teachings

1. THE SACRAMENTS HAVE BEEN INSTITUTED BY CHRIST

This is found in the Council of Trent, *Decree on the Sacraments,* sacraments in general, can. 1: "If anyone says that all the sacraments of the new law were not all instituted by our Lord Jesus Christ . . . let that person be anathema."

COMMENTS

1. The central issue, which the bishops at Trent wanted to define, in this particular teaching, was that *sacraments are primarily gifts of God.* Basically, sacraments are not of human origin; rather, sacraments are gifts from a loving and caring God. What God has done for us and is doing for us—the grace-filled kindness of God—is at the center of all sacramental life, and it is this emphasis which religious education teachers should emphasize again and again. Not what we do—for example, our preparation, our prayer, our worthiness—but what God first does on behalf of us should be the major focus in sacramental religious education.

2. In this teaching, the Roman Catholic Church has defined that Jesus *as God* instituted the sacraments. It is not part of Roman Catholic defined faith that Jesus *as a human being* instituted them. Religious education teachers can, of course, teach that Jesus instituted an individual sacrament at a given time in his life, e.g., baptism on the occasion of his own baptism, or the eucharist on the occasion of the last supper, but a teacher must also realize that pinpointing an exact time in the life of Jesus, in which the historical Jesus, acting in and through his humanity, is said to have instituted a given sacrament, is only a theological opinion, not part of defined Catholic doctrine.

3. **Relationship to Christian spirituality.** How can teachers unite this official statement: "Sacraments have been instituted by God," with Christian spirituality? The nourishing, spiritual depth of this small statement lies in our belief that God has taken the initiative. Sacraments are occasions of grace, occasions of God's free and unmerited gifts to us. Behind the technical term "institution of the sacraments," there is a profound spiritual meaning—it is God and God alone, who has freely given us love and mercy, presence and care. In our sacramental celebration, then, what we ourselves do is simply a response to what God has first done. As the letter of John [4:19] states: "We are able to love, because God first loved us." Religious education on the sacraments must begin and end with this deep but humbling belief that God, in the sacraments, first loves us. What we do in each of the sacraments is fundamentally a response to this compassionate, caring and undeserved love of God.

2. SACRAMENTS ARE SYMBOLS OF SOMETHING SACRED, AND THEY CONFER THE GRACE THEY SIGNIFY

This can be found in the Council of Trent, *Decree on the Sacraments,* sacraments in general, can. 7: "If anyone says that the sacraments of the new law do not contain the grace which they signify, or that they do not confer this grace to those who present no obstacle . . . let that person be anathema."

COMMENTS

1. The central issue of this defined teaching of the church focuses on the grace reality or the holiness which is at the heart of every sacramental action. In the celebration of each sacrament, the Christian community is celebrating the transcendent gift of God: first of all and primarily, the gift of God's own holy presence and life; secondly, the effects which God's holy presence therefore has on our own Christian lives, making our lives holy. In this sense, there is a real presence of the Lord in every sacrament, not simply a real presence of Jesus only in the eucharistic sacrament. The church is teaching us that the very holiness of God, namely, the very presence of God, is active in every sacramental action.

2. As signs and symbols, sacraments confer grace. Only this quite general statement, namely, that sacraments confer grace is the solemn teaching of the church.

That sacraments confer grace has been defined.

How sacraments confer or cause grace has not been defined.

Theologians, particularly Dominicans and Franciscans, have presented very different views on the way in which a sacrament confers grace. Dominican theologians, following Thomas Aquinas, explain the causality of grace through a theological view called "instrumental efficient causality." In this Thomistic view, the words of a priest [as also the matter and form] are considered "efficient instruments" used by God to produce grace. Franciscan theologians considered this efficient causality view to be a denial of God's freedom. God does not have to use any "instruments" to give grace, and if God does use created things like priestly words, bread, wine, oil, etc., they cannot be seen as "causing grace," since grace is an absolutely free gift. Franciscan theologians explained the causality of sacramental grace in two different ways: one group, following Bonaventure, considered all the human elements (words of a priest, bread and wine, etc.) to be "moral causes," similar to a prayer which asks God to freely give grace. The second group of Franciscan theologians, following John Duns Scotus, taught that sacraments "give" grace because of "occasional causality." When a community of Christians celebrates eucharist in the way God has instructed us to do, God, on that occasion, gives grace, not because of anything Christians do, but basically because God promised to give his grace on such occasions. It is the promise of God, not the words of a priest nor the use of correct materials, which is the basis for sacramental grace. Other theologians, particularly Jesuits, have refined or nuanced one or the other of these theological views when they try to explain the meaning of the phrase: "sacraments confer the grace they signify." A religious education teacher should make it clear that only the general notion, "sacraments truly do confer or cause grace" is the defined teaching of the church. A more precise description of the way in which this conferring or causing of grace takes place should be presented to students as a theological view or opinion. Students should be aware that none of these explanations of sacramental causality are the official teaching of the church.

3. Three different religious truths are intertwined in this official teaching of the church:

a. It is God who acts through the sacraments to give grace.
b. Christians can set up obstacles to grace (i.e., sin).
c. The sacraments confer the grace they signify.

The official teaching of the church does not attempt to explain in any detail how these three ideas can be put together. In their effort to unify these issues, theologians have offered a number of views. That these three truths are to be held as official and solemn is a teaching of the Roman Catholic Church. How these three truths are unified is not a teaching of the Roman Catholic Church.

4. Relationship to Christian spirituality. "Sacraments confer grace" is clearly a Christian belief which nourishes our spirituality in a very deep way. Grace, first of all, is a relationship, not a thing. Grace is God personally relating to each of us. This loving relationship of God to us takes place in many ways, not just in the sacraments. As a Christian community, however, we come together to celebrate this loving relationship of God to us in sacramental rituals and the community celebration reminds us that God loves us, not merely God loves me. There are no "personal" or "private" sacraments. There are only communal or social sacraments. One person alone never celebrates a sacrament; it is only a gathered group or community which celebrates a sacrament.

This social or communal dimension of sacramental life has profound spiritual implications. The gospels tell us to love our neighbor as we love ourselves; to ask God to forgive us our personal sins in the measure that we forgive others. Again and again we are asked to love. First of all, we are asked to love ourselves. When we love ourselves, we have a good self-image. In the sacramental celebrations, we are celebrating the most profound reason we have for loving ourselves, for having a good self-image: namely, that God first loves me. I am someone who is lovable. I am loved not simply by my parents, by my spouse, by my children and by my friends, but the all holy God finds me lovable. Moreover, God forgives me my sins: my worst sins, my hidden sins, my frequent sins. God loves and forgives me. When I share in a sacramental celebration with others, I praise and thank this God who loves and forgives me. But I am celebrating with others, whom God also loves and forgives, and if God can love them and forgive them, then I, too, must make every effort to love them and try to forgive them. Sacraments confer grace to me, and sacraments also confer grace to them. This means that God loves me, and that God loves them; that God forgives me, and that God forgives them. In all of this, we find the deepest meaning of sacramental spirituality. Be perfect as God is perfect; be compassionate as God is compassionate. In our efforts to be like God, we too must love and be compassionate, with ourselves and with others. Sacraments, by their very nature, are socially spiritual, never just privately spiritual.

3. THERE ARE SEVEN SACRAMENTS

This is found in the Council of Trent, *Decree on the Sacraments,* sacraments in general, can. 1, which lists all seven sacraments by name: baptism, confirmation eucharist, penance, extreme unction, order and matrimony. Each of these are defined as true and proper sacraments of the Roman Catholic Church.

COMMENTS

1. Almost every religious educator in North America today will have read some book dealing with the history of the sacraments. It was only from about 1950 onward, however, that in North American seminaries the theology of sacraments began to be taught in an historical way, and only in the twentieth century itself have the various histories of the individual sacraments been technically developed. In the light of the history of sacraments in the Roman Catholic Church, it is impossible to state that the church has "always taught" that there are seven sacraments. Prior to 1150 there was no teaching about "seven sacraments." This is most clear because of marriage. From about 1100 onward, the issue of marriage as a sacrament started to be discussed by theologians and canonists. At first, most theologians and canonists of that time refused to consider marriage a sacrament, since, as they argued, all sacraments give grace but marriage involves sex, which these same scholars considered to be at least venially sinful. They argued: How can anything sinful give grace? The theological and canonical documentation of this period of time makes it amply clear that this was the precise issue which blocked marriage from any consideration as a sacrament of the church. From 1150 onward, this gradually changed. Theologians and canonists arrived at a theological distinction which allowed marriage, understood as a contract or as an interpersonal consent, to give grace, leaving the actual sexual aspect of marriage to one side. Only then was marriage considered a sacrament and, when this happened, theologians and canonists began to speak about the "seven sacraments." Within a very short time, this teaching of seven sacraments began to appear in official church documents, and the bishops at the Council of Trent made this teaching solemnly official.

Historically, one also finds problems with confirmation. When did the Western church begin to consider confirmation as a sacrament? Prior to the year 1000, the data for the sacramentality of confirmation becomes increasingly rare. Only from 1000 onward can one say that a separate rite of confirmation was the general practice in the West, but not in the East. Likewise, the sacramentality of penance cannot be established with any certainty prior to 150, nor is there any sure data on a ritual of ordination prior to 200. Today, this kind of historical material is well-known to every religious education teacher. Because of these historical facts, the question immediately arises: In what way, then, can one teach that there is a dogma of the church regarding the seven sacraments?

Since the vast amount of material on the history of the sacraments is fairly new, theologians have not yet fully integrated the historical data with this dogma of the church. Some theologians have utilized the issue of development of doctrine, and undoubtedly something along this line will have to be involved as the resolution of this matter becomes clearer. But as yet a satisfactory integration of the historical data and the "seven sacrament" teaching has not been fully developed. The issue is compounded even more by the teaching of Vatican II, that the church itself is a basic sacrament, and also by the teaching of reputable Roman Catholic theologians that Jesus, in his humanity, is the primordial sacrament. One could even say that these positions indicate that there are now "nine sacraments" not seven.

2. Vatican II officially teaches that the church itself is a sacrament, indeed a basic sacrament. That the church is a basic sacrament is part of the ordinary magisterium of the church, since it was stated so strongly and so often in the documents of Vatican II. Moreover, respected Roman Catholic theologians such as Karl Rahner and Edward Schillebeeckx and many others also teach that Jesus, in his humanity, is the basic or most fundamental sacrament. This teaching on Jesus is, of course, a theological view; it has not been officially adopted by the episcopal magisterium. Both teachings, namely the church as a fundamental sacrament and Jesus as the most basic sacrament, are new insights in sacramental theology. Contemporary theologians have attempted to relate the official teaching on seven sacraments with this new approach of two additional sacraments: namely, Jesus and church as fundamental sacraments. At this particular period of time, religious education teachers should indeed mention that besides the traditional seven sacraments, the bishops at Vatican II have officially taught that the church itself is a fundamental sacrament and that many contemporary Roman Catholic theologians teach that Jesus is the most fundamental sacrament of all. Teachers should also indicate that the relationship between the teaching of seven sacraments and the teaching of these two fundamental sacraments is still being developed by various theologians. To date, every position remains merely a theological opinion.

   3. Relationship to Christian spirituality. What is the spiritual meaning behind this statement of faith: "There are seven sacraments"? From the Council of Trent to Vatican II, the major spiritual aspect of this teaching was, more often than not, to reconfirm us in our Roman Catholic faith, with its belief in seven sacraments, over against a Protestant faith with its belief in only two sacraments. By our belief in this teaching of the church, we were strengthened in our belief that we were truly followers of Jesus and truly participants in the one true church. This was an apologetic form of spirituality. However, there is a deeper spiritual meaning than this when one joins this statement of seven sacraments to the current theological understanding that Jesus himself, in his humanity, is the most fundamental sacrament and to the teaching of Vatican II that the church itself is a basic sacrament. Jesus, the sacrament of our encounter with God, is the way Schillebeeckx expressed this approach, and this means that in each sacramental celebration we encounter God. We experience a spiritual moment when God is really present to us. We do not see or experience God directly, but in a sacramental way. This teaching on the seven sacraments helps us spiritually, since in each sacramental celebration we encounter the "real presence" of God.

   There is, as well, an encounter with the church as a fundamental sacrament. In the baptism ritual, for instance, we experience the sacrament called church and this church-sacrament in turn points us to Jesus. In this baptismal ritual, we also experience the real presence of Jesus, the most fundamental sacrament of all, but Jesus in and through his humanity points to a loving, compassionate God. Sacraments are signs **of** something and **to** someone. In the signing, however, sacraments also bring about a reality: (a) the real presence of oneself and one's community to God; and more importantly, (b) God's real presence to one's community and to one's self. It is *the spiritual encounter with the real presence of Jesus*—a real presence not only in eucharist but in all seven sacraments—which makes the seven-fold teaching about sacraments profoundly spiritual. Enriched by the addition of two foundational sacraments: the church and the humanity of Jesus, all of the seven sacramental rituals are moments when an individual Christian and the Christian community itself are brought into the very meaning of all sacraments: a sacramental encounter with God. The fundamental, basic, primordial sacrament, namely, Jesus, is really present in every sacramental experience and is our sacramental encounter with God. As this new insight into the very meaning of sacramentality continues to develop in the Roman Catholic Church, the spiritual depth of each of the seven sacraments will also be enriched, and it is in this area, still somewhat in process, from which a religious education teacher can draw out the spirituality of the teaching on seven sacraments.

4. THREE SACRAMENTS CONFER A CHARACTER: HOLY BAPTISM, HOLY CONFIRMATION AND HOLY ORDER

This is found in the Council of Trent, *Decree on the Sacraments,* sacraments in general, can. 9: "If anyone says that in three sacraments, namely baptism, confirmation and order, a character, that is a certain spiritual and indelible sign, is not imprinted on the soul, so that these sacraments cannot be repeated, let that person be anathema."

COMMENTS

1. The central focus of this official and solemn teaching of the church is this: that there are three sacraments which confer a character is the defined teaching of the church; what this character is has never been defined by the church. There are, however, many theological views on "what" this character is. The major issue behind this teaching is stated in the canon from Trent cited above: namely, these three sacraments are not to be repeated. If in religious education the idea that there is some indelible marking on the soul and this is described in any detail, one has entered the area of theological opinion: the "what" this character might be. No "what" can ever be presented as the "official" teaching of the church. Essentially, this teaching centers on one major issue: namely, not repeating these sacraments during one's lifetime here on earth.

2. As regards this issue of sacramental character, baptism and confirmation must be understood in a unified way, almost as a single sacrament, since the historical reason why confirmation is said to confer a character is due *to its intrinsic connection to baptism.* The major focus of this teaching on character centers, therefore, on the non-repetition of two sacraments: baptism and order. Confirmation is added, but only because of baptism.

3. Relationship to Christian spirituality. When the church community celebrates baptism, it is celebrating God who so loves us that God gives us a share in divine life itself. We call this baptismal grace. During our entire lifetime, God will never disown our baptism. We will always be God's baptized child. Likewise, when one is ordained, God will never disown the ordained person during the remainder of his lifetime. Throughout one's entire lifetime, the ordained person will always be God's deacon, God's priest, God's bishop. This fidelity of God to us, either as a baptized Christian or as an ordained minister of the Christian community, is the spiritual depth which should be stressed again and again. God loves us with an "everlasting" love, and in the sacraments of baptism, confirmation and order the Christian community celebrates this "everlasting" love. Nonetheless, the spiritual stress should be on the phrase, "in our lifetime," much more than on the term "everlasting." Sacraments are a fundamental part of our church life on this earth. The teaching on "sacramental character" focuses primarily on our ecclesial life here on earth. Whenever we go beyond our present life and speculate about heaven, i.e., will baptism-confirmation remain operative in heaven, will people still be deacons, priests and bishops in heaven, more often than not, we enter into the area of theological opinion. Just as the definition of sacramental character centers on never repeating these three sacraments during one's entire lifetime, so, too, the spiritual understanding of sacramental character should center primarily on the meaning of sacramental character during one's lifetime here on earth, namely, that God will never disown us during our earthly life. Teachers should not enter into descriptions of how this teaching on sacramental character may affect our heavenly life.

5. GOD'S ACTION IN THE SACRAMENTS DOES NOT DEPEND ON THE INTENTION OR HOLINESS OF THE MINISTER

This is found in the Council of Trent, *Decree on the Sacraments,* sacraments in general, can. 11 and 12. One cannot deny that a minister who intends to do what the church does is not a real minister of the sacrament; nor can one deny that a minister, in the state of serious sin, cannot truly minister the sacraments.

COMMENTS

1. Behind this solemn teaching of the church one finds centuries of dispute and controversy. Again and again, individual or regional Christian communities would not accept sacraments celebrated by unworthy bishops or unworthy priests. These communities simply called such "sacramental actions" null and void. In their view only holy bishops and holy priests and holy deacons could celebrate "true" sacraments. Even popes were not always clear on this issue, with some popes demanding holiness and orthodox faith for true sacramental validity, and other popes not demanding such holiness or orthodox faith. We still find today some individual Christians, as well as some Christian communities, who will only accept or acknowledge other individual Christians and other Christian communities who measure up to their definition of the "holy" or who profess their understanding of "orthodox faith." All who are not "holy" in their understanding of the term, or all who do not hold "orthodox faith" in their understanding of the term, have been called, at times, diabolical, evil, non-Christian, satanic, anti-Christ, etc. Even Roman Catholic communities used such names for those sacramental ministers they did not consider either holy or orthodox. At the time of the Council of Trent, there were Protestant groups, including at times their bishops and priests, who did not believe the same way that Roman Catholics did. If their bishops, priests and deacons did not have the "true" faith, could they celebrate the sacraments validly? If they had married and were living in sin, could they celebrate the sacraments validly? These issues were very real for the bishops at Trent. After much discussion, the official and defined teaching of the Roman Catholic Church was this: In a given sacrament, if one at least intends to do what the church itself intends, the sacramental action is valid, provided the minister is a valid minister of the sacrament. If a bishop, priest or deacon celebrates a sacrament while in the "state of sin," the sacrament is valid. Unless one has some understanding of the centuries-long fight over these issues, one might not understand the focus of this teaching. By making the Roman Catholic position regarding both the intention and the holiness of the minister clear, the leadership of the church officially brought to an end centuries of bitter struggle. This was, however, only an "official ending" of this struggle. In the practical order, the struggle over these very same issues can be found even in our own day and age.

2. Relationship to Christian spirituality. Spiritually, the depth in this solemn teaching is its focus on the unending mercy and love of God. The spiritual focus should not be on the minister's intentions nor on his holiness. When one begins to see that God acts, sometimes in spite of the bishop, in spite of the priest, or in spite of the deacon, then one begins to see how deeply God truly operates on our behalf in each and every sacramental celebration. Not even a muddled intention by a bishop, priest or deacon is stronger than God. Not even the immorality of a bishop, priest or deacon can stop the power of God's compassionate love for us as we celebrate a sacrament. Once again, sacraments are basically not something we do, nor something which church ministers do. Sacraments are celebrations of what God is doing in love, care, presence and compassion. When one, in a sacramental action, is spiritually stopped by a minister of little or no faith, when one is put off by an immoral deacon, priest or bishop, one has not plumbed the spiritual depths of a sacramental celebration. After all, we are all sinful people, including bishops, priests and deacons, but together as a community we celebrate the sacraments of the church. We might even be called at times a sinful church, but we continue to celebrate the holy mysteries which God has given us. In God's eyes, we do not have to be perfect first and only then celebrate these mysteries. Paul himself writes in Romans that God loved us and justified us, when we were still in sin. So, too, it is because we are imperfect and sinful people that we celebrate God's sacraments. When we begin to realize this, we begin to see the height and depth, the breadth and the length of the mercy and compassion of God: neither our imperfections, nor the imperfections of our ordained ministers can ever outstrip the merciful love of God.

These five issues are key to every catechesis on the sacraments and should be central to every syllabus of a religious education teacher. There are, however, other teachings on sacraments which are official and currently central.

Sacraments in General
Teachings of the Ordinary Magisterium

The main documentation of the "ordinary magisterium" of the church, which affects a general teaching on sacramental theology is: [1] the various documents of Vatican II; [2] the new sacramental rituals developed after Vatican II; and [3] the code of canon law which was revised in 1983.

When the various committees worked on the revision of the sacramental rituals, they found in the documents of Vatican II criteria which they used as the framework for their revisions. These criteria, expressed clearly in the documents themselves, indicate the ordinary magisterium's approach to a general view of sacramental theology and liturgy today.

Sacraments in General
General Criteria

On the basis of statements made in the documents of Vatican II, the following criteria have served as the guiding principles or general criteria for the renewal of the sacramental rites. All the committees, which have worked on these renewed rituals, took these criteria into account.

1. "Liturgical services are not private functions but are celebrations of the church, which is the sacrament of unity, namely, the holy people united and gathered under their bishops." (*SC* 26; cf. also 27, 28, 29, 30, 31 and 32) It is abundantly clear that the celebration of the sacraments is communal, not private; indeed, the more involved the people of God are in the celebration of the sacraments, the better the sacramental liturgy becomes. The more privatized or individualized a sacramental liturgy becomes, the less perfect it is. This is repeated in canon law, can. 837.

2. "The rites should be distinguished by a noble simplicity. They should be short, clear and free from useless repetitions. They should be within the people's powers of comprehension and normally should not require much explanation." (*SC* 34) Sacramental celebrations should be clear, non-repetitive, and simple. The more complicated and repetitive liturgical celebrations become, the less liturgical they really are.

3. "In sacred celebrations a more ample, more varied and more suitable reading from sacred scripture should be restored." (*SC* 35) In celebrating each sacrament, there should be a reading from the scriptures. The role of the Word of God is given a greater position and presence in the liturgy of the new sacramental rituals than one finds in the former sacramental rituals. Liturgies, with no proclamation of the Word of God, are not good liturgies.

4. "A sermon is part of the liturgical action . . . the sermon should draw its content mainly from scriptural and liturgical sources." (*SC* 35) A homily is clearly part of every sacramental celebration. This accords well with the statement, often found in official church documents, that the most important task of a priest is to preach the Word of God.

5. "In liturgical celebrations each person, minister or layman who has an office to perform should carry out all and only those parts which pertain to his office by the nature of the rite and the norms of the liturgy." (*SC* 28) Because the new sacramental rituals are celebrations of a Christian community, the celebrations have ministerial presiders. The bishop, priest or deacon, when they preside, are the main ministerial presiders. However, they are not the only ministerial presiders during a sacramental liturgy, since there are "ministers of the Word," who proclaim the scriptures to the people; there are ministers of prayer, who lead the community in specific petitions; there are eucharistic ministers, who communicate the gathered community. There are ministers of music, namely the choir. On the occasion of their specific function, they are at that moment the main presiders of the sacramental liturgy. Through the minister of the Word, for instance, all of the gathered Christians, including a presiding bishop, priest or deacon, are at that moment listeners to the Word of God, which is being proclaimed to them through the minister of the Word. In post-Vatican II sacramental liturgies, there is no longer a single minister but a plurality of ministers during each sacramental celebration. "The proclamation of God's word and our response of faith express the celebration's meaning." [*Catechism* 1190]

6. The role of the church is emphasized, not simply the role of the priest or the role of the recipient. The role of the gathered community is to be ritually visual. Canon law mentions that the sacraments are the "actions of Christ and the church." (Can. 840) Good liturgy will include this ritual visibility of the entire people of God; poor liturgy will diminish the ritual visibility of the entire people of God. In the official documents, no mention is made of the ritual visibility of a male/female church community. When a liturgy has a ritual visibility of only men, something is lacking in a sacramental ritual, which is meant to be the celebration of the entire people of God.

7. "Whenever necessity requires or genuine advantage suggests . . . it is lawful for the faithful for whom it is physically or morally impossible to approach a Catholic minister, to receive the sacraments of penance, eucharist and anointing of the sick from non-Catholic ministers in whose churches these sacraments are valid." (Can. 844) It is important to see that, in the teaching of the ordi-

nary magisterium, the validity of sacraments is not limited only to
the Roman Catholic Church. This is especially stated for penance,
eucharist and anointing of the sick, but by saying this, there is
also an acknowledgement of the validity of holy order in these
churches, and an acceptance of the sacramental marriages, which
have duly taken place in these same churches. Moreover, Catholic
ministers may administer penance, eucharist and anointing of the
sick to members of the oriental churches, even though they do not
have "full communion" with the Roman Catholic Church. (Can.
844) This reciprocal action is an acknowledgement of the baptism,
eucharist, legitimate ordination, and valid sacramental marriages
of members of the various Eastern churches. No requirement is
made that these non-uniate, Eastern rite Christians must acknowledge the pope prior to the reception of eucharist, penance or
anointing. This situation, of course, raises major questions on the
very meaning of "full communion."

8. Both the decree on the liturgy and the code of canon law state
clearly that only proper church authority can determine the rules
for the celebration of official liturgical actions, especially the sacramental actions. Cf. *SC* 22, 23, 37, 38, 39, 40; canon law, can.
841, 846. However, in the decree on the liturgy, the bishops also
stated very clearly that adaptations can and should be made because of cultural differences (*SC* 37, 38, 39, 40). The bishops at
Vatican II clearly wanted to open the doors to more culturally
sensitive celebrations of the sacraments. This follows from the
bishops' emphasis on the sacraments as celebrations of a gathered
Christian community; on the role of the vernacular; and on the
involvement of a variety of ministers. Reluctance to be sensitive
to cultural ways of celebrating sacraments is not in accord with
the express criteria established by the bishops of Vatican II. Such
a reluctance goes against the ordinary magisterium of the church.

9. "Even in the liturgy the church does not wish to impose a rigid
uniformity in matters which do not involve the faith of the good
of the whole community." (*SC* 37) This same conciliar document
explains this statement (37–40) by stressing the inculturation and
acculturation which should be part of liturgical and sacramental
renewal, even stating that at times a "radical adaptation of the
liturgy" might be needed (40). Monolithic liturgy and liturgies

which do not reflect cultural differences are not sound sacramental liturgies.

These are all major issues of the ordinary magisterium of the church which should be a part of any course on Christian sacraments. None of these issues should be presented as infallibly defined teachings of the church, but they should be seen as the official and currently normative positions of church leadership. These norms and criteria did not necessarily govern the way sacraments were celebrated in past centuries of Christian life, and these norms and criteria can be changed in future revisions of the sacramental rites. However, they are the official criteria now and must be respected by all Catholics.

In religious education classes, students may hear, discuss and understand these regulations. However, when these same students attend sacramental celebrations in their parish churches, such as the Sunday liturgy or the sacrament of reconciliation, they may find that certain pastors are reluctant to follow these criteria, or follow them only in a minimal way. This can and does happen even though the bishop of the diocese continually urges the renewal of liturgy according to the regulations of Vatican II and canon law. When the students return to the religious education class and bring up this kind of discrepancy, what can the religious education teacher do? To criticize such a pastor only engenders a totally new set of problems. To excuse the pastor, because he is old or ill, only delays the resolution of the problem. To advise the students to find another parish, more open to the regulations and directions of the ordinary magisterium, can cause dissension in the family. There is a major dilemma here for a religious educator. It is clear that the real issue is not in the church's doctrine [ordinary magisterium] nor in the religious education classes. The real issue is the pastor who does not want to support legitimate church directives. He does this quite often by passive resistance. Such a pastor has willingly accepted his role as a public person in the church (*persona publica in ecclesia*), but he refuses to accept the consequences. The publication of the *Catechism of the Catholic Church* is a "wake-up" call to such pastors, reminding them that it is the proper and legitimate role of church authority—here the bishops, the popes, the conference of bishops—to establish the regulations, and both the decree on the sacred liturgy in Vatican II and the code of canon law referred to above in no. 8 do not empower a pastor to do whatever he prefers on the issue of sacramental celebrations. Reluctant pastors, who refuse to accept the teachings of the ordinary magisterium of the church on sacramental and liturgical issues, do as much harm, if not more harm, to the Catholic

Church than the so-called liberal priests and lay people who are said to "do whatever they want" during a sacramental celebration. Are not reluctant pastors doing "whatever they want" as well?

Sacraments in General
A Celebration of the Church's Liturgy

A key word which many use to tie sacramental theology, liturgy and canon law together is: celebrate. Who celebrates? How do we celebrate? When do we celebrate? Where do we celebrate? What do we celebrate? This final question is the key for all the others. The answer to the question: what do we celebrate? is clearly this—we celebrate that God has first loved us. Who, when, how and where are meaningful questions, only if there is a primary and fundamental reason for celebration, and that primary, fundamental reason is God's action, not ours. This "what-do-we-celebrate" aspect of celebration governs all other aspects of celebrating sacraments.

The four foundational issues mentioned above as regards all sacramental and liturgical worship help a teacher answer the question: what do we celebrate?

a. God's action is primary;
b. the Christo-centrism of all liturgy;
c. the role of the Holy Spirit;
d. the celebration is an action of the whole Christ, *Christus totus,* Jesus and the worshipping community.

Religious education teachers know well that whatever one presents as the basic or foundational ideas of a given subject must be clearly evident and integrated when a particularized development of that subject is made. Otherwise, the purpose of the general presentation of basic and foundational material becomes questionable. Profoundly embedded in these foundational ideas is the action of God. This is indeed foundationally what we celebrate in each and every sacrament.

On the basis of the key idea of "what" we celebrate, there is a second major idea. Since it is the whole Christ who primarily celebrates in each and every liturgy, it is insufficient to say that it is the bishop/priest/deacon who celebrates. This person may, indeed, be the main presider or celebrant, but he is not the only celebrant, and he is not even the "main" celebrant, since the "main" celebrant is the whole Christ, *Christus totus,* the entire community gathered around Christ. As such, the entire community with Christ himself is the "main celebrant." Obviously, the role of the ordained minister must be somewhat reconsidered, given this communal approach to liturgical actions.

The basis for this communal celebration is this: *all Christians have the right and duty to be an active participant in liturgical celebrations by reason of their baptism.* The magisterial teaching of chapter three in *Lumen Gentium* on the people of God assures us that this is a matter of profound importance. The right and duty of liturgical ministry, which one has in virtue of holy baptism, is doctrinally of key importance. The bishops at Vatican II, in the construction of *Lumen Gentium,* deliberately placed chapter two, on the "people of God," with its resounding statements on the priesthood of all Christians and the ministry in the church which comes from baptism. These same bishops deliberately postponed the issue of the hierarchical church to chapter three so as to relate hierarchy into a more baptismal ecclesiology. In baptism, each Christian shares in the threefold mission and ministry of Jesus. This is a doctrinally major issue which all religious education teachers must emphasize. Moreover, the commissioning of each and every baptized person to such mission and ministry comes originally from the Lord himself, not from the hierarchy and not from the community.

The other questions: "how," "when" and "where" the community celebrates, involve a great variety of issues of lesser moment: altars, tabernacles, chrism, chairs and lecterns, on the one hand; Sundays, feast days, and the hours of the divine office, on the other. Images, music, words and actions also enter the picture. Too often, lengthy descriptions of these lesser, but more concrete and picturesque issues, tend to make the foundational elements fade, while matters of lesser moment begin to receive more and more focus. A religious education teacher does well to make sure that the reasons why there are altars, tabernacles, chrism, etc., etc., are clear:

1. the Christian community is celebrating what God has first done for us;
2. that the liturgy primarily celebrates the paschal mystery by which Christ saved us;
3. that the liturgy celebrates the action of the Holy Spirit;
4. that it is the whole Christ, the *Christus totus,* who is the primary celebrant in each sacramental ritual.

Pedagogically, one must continue to go back to these four foundational ideas, lest the students become so enamored with issues of secondary moment that the primary issues become non-operative.

Sacraments in General
Unresolved Issues

In the actual life of the church not everything can be brought together into an organic synthesis. As regards sacramental teaching there might even be a misleading sense of a serenely unified doctrine, of an organically well-synthesized corpus of liturgical and sacramental material. In reading certain books on the sacraments one might even get the impression that there are no serious problems. Theologically, this is not the case. There *are* areas of sacramental thought which remain unresolved. Pedagogically, these areas of unresolved situations must be presented as open questions. If this is not done, religious education students will eventually realize that the sacramental doctrine which they had learned is not the serene and unified picture which they had been taught. There are clearly issues, many of them quite serious, which are unresolved and should never be taught as resolved issues. As regards the general overview of liturgical and sacramental theology, the key current unresolved issues include the following.

1. GOD'S ACTION IN THE SACRAMENTS

There is need for much more clarity in sacramental liturgy, doctrine and spirituality on the issue that God's action is primary, and all other actions, personal and ecclesial, are secondary. In the areas of both spirituality and doctrine, an overstress on human action can conflict with the decree on justification promulgated by the Council of Trent, which states clearly that God's action is primary.

2. THE REAL PRESENCE OF JESUS

The real presence of Jesus in the liturgy and in all sacraments, not simply a "real" presence of Jesus in the eucharist, remains an unresolved issue. The theological interrelationship of these aspects of real presence has not yet been totally developed. Both the *Constitution on the Sacred Liturgy,* promulgated by Vatican II, and the encyclical *Mysterium fidei* by Paul VI refer to a multiple-use of the term "real presence." Paul VI says that Jesus is really present in the church when it prays; in the church as it performs works of mercy; in the church in its pilgrimage of struggle to reach the harbor of eternal life; in the church as it preaches; in the church as it governs the people of God; in the church as it offers in his name the sacrifice of the mass; in the church as it administers the sacraments. How all these real presences of Jesus in the church can be brought into a unified format remains an unresolved issue. Religious educators will simply have to acknowledge this unresolution and present it as such to their students.

3. JESUS AND CHURCH: FUNDAMENTAL SACRAMENTS

The theology of the church as a "basic sacrament" and Jesus as a "fundamental sacrament" and the seven sacraments are new ideas. The tensions in this interrelationship have not been fully resolved, and the approach by "analogy" remains only one of several theologically competing views. In many books on sacramental theology, various attempts to incorporate the sacramentality of Jesus and the sacramentality of the church have been tried. In other books on the sacraments, including the new catechism, the authors have made little or no effort to integrate these issues—one of which comes from Vatican II itself—into their presentation of the various sacraments. The issue is unresolved. Religious education teachers, however, would be well-advised to make as much effort as they can to incorporate the church as a basic sacrament into their own presentations, since this teaching is clearly part of the ordinary magisterium of the church. To go further and incorporate Jesus as the most fundamental sacrament is also helpful, even though this has not been officially taught by the hierarchical magisterium.

4. CELEBRATION BY THE ENTIRE CHRISTIAN COMMUNITY

The whole community, the body of Christ united to its Head, celebrates sacramental liturgy. The new catechism uses the term, *Totus Christus,* the entire Christ, which is both Jesus and the worshipping community. The relationship of the community as the whole Christ who celebrates, and the ordained minister as the sacramental presider, is still being worked out theologically. On this issue, there are, at present, strongly held theological positions which are not serenely or organically unified, primarily because the issue of clerical ordination has not been totally resolved. The relationship of the priesthood of all believers, a term which both the documents of Vatican II and the code of canon law use, to the ordained priesthood has, as yet, not been clearly settled. The resolution of this issue appears to be one which will take a long, long time to unravel.

5. CULTURE AND SACRAMENTAL CELEBRATIONS

Within today's Roman Catholic Church there are serious clashes in liturgy and sacramental celebration over the issue of culture. There is no synthesis on this matter as yet, and the idea that all legitimate rites today are of *equal value* is not that well honored in either theory or in practice. As long as liturgical rituals and their underlying theology remain basically Anglo-American/European, there will be little resolution to this issue. However, the culture issue goes far beyond sacramental theology and includes such issues as an understanding of the meaning of a human person, one's basic philosophy and epistemology, the meaning of symbol in one's life, the approach to authority, etc. Because of this web of issues, the many cultural issues will also take time to resolve.

3

The Sacrament of Holy Baptism

Christian initiation involves baptism, confirmation and eucharist. For a religious educator this is an extremely important issue, since a theological explanation of baptism which is not at the same time eucharistic (and confirmational) is insufficient, and a theological explanation of eucharist that is not at the same time baptismal (and confirmational) is also insufficient. The three sacraments form a unity of sacramental initiation. A mere presentation of these three sacraments in a given chronological order, namely, baptism, confirmation, and eucharist, is neither theologically nor pedagogically adequate to explain the full interrelationship of these sacramental realities of Christian initiation. Baptism is intrinsically eucharistic, and eucharist is intrinsically baptismal, so that the one cannot be understood nor explained without the other.

In current sacramental literature, there are several books that deal with the history of the sacrament of baptism. Often, this historical data is an excellent pedagogical way to begin, since the history helps to situate more meaningfully the present ritual of baptism. I have found that the majority of my own students are not turned off by the history of the sacraments; quite the contrary, a careful presentation of such a history answers many of their questions about a given sacrament.

There are also many well-crafted works on the biblical data regarding baptism, which a religious education teacher will find of value to clarify New Testament texts on baptism. Sound historical and biblical material are of considerable pedagogical value, since the use of such data assists one to distinguish certain statements about biblical and historical issues, which one can make with full or almost full assurance. Moreover, there are certain statements about the biblical and historical understanding of baptism that can be made, but only with moderate or limited assurance.

There are positions on the biblical and historical understanding of baptism which one can make, but only in a most tentative way. Finally, there are biblical and historical conclusions which one should never draw, since the historical and biblical material offers no support for such views. In this latter category, unfortunately, there have been, and still are, many "popular" views of biblical interpretation and historical explanation regarding baptism which are today untenable.

Second, an explanation of the current ritual of baptism offers a valuable approach to the meaning of baptism. It is well to recall, however, that no book, not even a ritual, adequately contains the meaning of baptism. Baptism is a process and an action-event. It is only in the actual celebration of baptism that one truly finds the reality of baptism. All books and all educational materials are simply pointers to a reality, never found adequately portrayed in the abstractions of a book.

The *Rite of Christian Initiation of Adults (RCIA)* has been one of the most exciting and enriching results of the post-Vatican II sacramental renewal. The communities which have celebrated the lengthy process of the *RCIA* have again and again experienced in a most spiritual way the meaning of Christian initiation. Even though there is a book which contains the ritual of the *RCIA*, such a ritual is not the place in which the reality of baptism can be found. The *RCIA* is a liturgical and spiritual process, and it is only in the lived experience of this spiritual, liturgical and sacramental event, that the reality of baptism takes place.

The depths of this meaning in the *RCIA,* as also in the *Rite of Baptism for Children* and the more recent *Rite of Baptism for Children of Catechetical Age,* center around the following issues:

a. The celebration is primarily a celebration of what God has done and is doing and will continue to do in the lives of those involved. The celebration of Christian initiation is the celebration of God's free and unmerited grace. The response of the Christian individual and of the Christian community is always a matter of secondary importance.

b. The initiation liturgies celebrate, again in a primary way, the paschal mystery by which Christ saved us. We do not save ourselves; salvation, justification, sanctification, liberation are due entirely to the full efficacy of Jesus' paschal mystery.

c. The sacraments of initiation are celebrations of the action of the Holy Spirit within the community called church.

d. The entire Christ, the gathered and worshipping Christian community, are the primary celebrants of the sacraments of initiation. The sacraments of initiation are not celebrated primarily by clergy. The sacraments of initiation can only be understood, when they are experienced as celebrations, and the spirit of celebration should permeate the entire liturgical process.

The sacrament of the eucharist is an integral part of Christian initiation. Baptism and eucharist need to be interrelated, not only in practice, but also in the classroom. An explanation of this interrelationship of baptism to eucharist should focus on the most important aspect or the deepest core of both baptism and eucharist. The most important mystery in eucharistic theology, however, is not what we do, i.e., receive communion, but what God does. The most important eucharistic mystery is the real presence of Jesus, an unmerited gift of Jesus' own presence to a gathered community. The most profound moment in the liturgical eucharistic action is the eucharistic prayer, not the response of the Christian community in holy communion. A religious educator will have to flesh out the depth of the mystery of holy baptism as an action of God and its relationship to the mystery of holy eucharist in ways which truly unite the heart of baptism to the heart of eucharist. This profound relationship is not merely that baptism prepares us for first communion.

The integration of confirmation into the initiatory process is also important, but the connection of baptism/confirmation is not self-evident, particularly since confirmation in our American-European world occurs so long after the baptism of an infant and so long after the first communion of a child. In the *Rite of Baptism for Children of Catechetical Age* and the *Rite of Baptism for Adults,* baptism/confirmation/eucharist are all united in one liturgical act.

The following is a list of the most solemn and official teachings of the church as regards baptism. Religious educators will not present them precisely in this format, but somewhere in their course, these key issues will have to be included, and students will have to understand that these are the "immutable" aspects of baptismal theology.

The Sacrament of Holy Baptism
Defined Teaching

1. HOLY BAPTISM IS A SACRAMENT

This is found in the Council of Trent, *Decree on the Sacraments,* sacraments in general, can. 1, in which all seven sacraments are enumerated.

COMMENTS

1. The main issue in this defined doctrine is this: from the New Testament times onward, the Christian church has maintained in a consistent way that baptism is a fundamental and sacred ritual of the community.

2. Not all the Christian churches call this ritual a "sacrament." The precise name, *sacrament,* is not the focus of the definition. The Eastern churches for the most part refer to baptism as a "mystery." This term was used by Christians for baptism long before the Latin term, *sacramentum,* and consequently the term, mystery, is far more traditional than the term, sacrament. Moreover, among a number of Protestant churches, the term, ordinance, is used, based on Mt. 28:18–20, in which Jesus "orders" his followers to go, preach, and baptize. One of the main reasons why various Protestant groups do not use the term, sacrament, is their rejection of a seven-sacrament system as found in the Roman Catholic Church. Actually, the name is a secondary issue; the reality of the ritual is the primary issue.

3. Relationship to Christian spirituality. Religious education teachers can draw out the spiritual depths of this fairly wooden statement by relating it to the foundational elements. In the ritual of baptism, the community celebrates what God has done, is doing, and will continue to do for the one who is being baptized. This action of God becomes clearer when we relate this to Jesus' own baptism, when the heavens opened, the Spirit came down on Jesus, and God said, "This is my child." In each baptism, the heavens open, the Spirit comes down, and God says to the one who is baptized: This is my son. This is my daughter. I am well pleased. It is surely this loving action of God in Christ that we, the Christian community, celebrate in each and every baptism.

2. BAPTISM IS THE "FIRST" OF THE SACRAMENTS

In the history of the church, baptism has consistently been the first of the ritualized sacraments. Since there has never been any denial of this progression, no official defined church statement specifically addresses the issue of "first."

COMMENTS

1. Were one to celebrate baptism after eucharist, after confirmation, etc., not only the Roman Catholic Church, but all the Christian churches would disapprove. It is this consistency of theory and practice which is at the core of this official and solemn teaching.

2. Today, many renowned Roman Catholic theologians refer to

Jesus as the "first" sacrament, the primordial sacrament. The ordinary magisterium of the church at Vatican II has officially presented the church itself as the basic—and therefore in some way "first"—sacrament. The term, "first," when applied to baptism, means first among the ritualized sacraments. Both Jesus and the church itself can be seen as more fundamental sacraments and therefore have a priority or "firstness."

3. Relationship to Christian spirituality. It is certainly in and through the term, "first," that the spirituality of this aspect of baptism can be developed. The "first" can be understood as the start of a series: baptism, confirmation, etc. "First" can also be seen as the action of God. By relating this action of God to a theology of grace, a teacher can make this brief sentence quite meaningful, since God's grace is a gift, a first gift; it is free and unmerited; it is given without regard to our worthiness, indeed it is even given to us, in spite of our unworthiness. It is given to us first; only then can we and do we try to respond by a good Christian life.

3. BAPTISM WAS INSTITUTED BY JESUS

This can be found in the Council of Trent, *Decree on the Sacraments,* sacraments in general, can. 1: "If anyone says that the sacraments of the new law were not all instituted by Jesus Christ . . . let that person be anathema."

COMMENTS

1. The core of this official and solemn teaching is, once again, that the sacraments are from God, not human fabrications. Even though the church leadership has developed, changed and rearranged the various prayers and ritual actions of baptism, the spiritual core of the baptismal reality is God-given.

2. The definition does not state that Jesus, at a given moment of his public ministry, "instituted" the sacrament of baptism. Theologians have proposed many moments when he might have done this, but these are all theological opinions. None of them are the defined teaching of the church.

3. Relationship to Christian spirituality. The mystery of our redemption is totally the work of God in Jesus. In this sense, Jesus "institutes" our salvation. We do not save ourselves, but rather we are saved by the loving and compassionate grace of God. Whatever we do is but a response to this "institution" from the Lord. Considered from this basic viewpoint, spiritual exercises, e.g., prayer and good works, are responses to God's acts. The beginning of prayer is amazement, that is, when one stands back in wonder and awe at the immensity of God's love. Only when a person has caught some inkling of this wonderful love of God, will that person really understand the meaning of prayer. As teachers, then, we do all we can to present the height and depth, the length and width of the wonderful acts of God.

4. BAPTISM IS CELEBRATED WITH WATER

This is found in the Council of Trent, can. 2 on baptism, which rejects an understanding of baptismal water as merely a "metaphor." Actually, the use of water has been a consistent teaching of the entire Christian community from New Testament times onward.

COMMENTS

1. The only issue which is official and solemn is this: baptism includes real water. The manner in which the water is used, i.e., by immersion, sprinkling, or pouring on the forehead, is not part of the official teaching, and all three methods are acceptable.

2. In the history of the church, various other liquids were at times used for baptism, and immediately the question of a valid baptism arose. The same questioning occurred when no water was used for baptism, but only the words were used.

3. Relationship to Christian spirituality. Many spiritual books wax eloquent on the beauty of water. Many garner from both the Old and New Testament descriptions of water in the economy of salvation: the water in Genesis, the deluge at the time of Noah, the passage of the Jews through the Reed Sea, etc. Such analogies are very helpful, but the metaphorical and mythological overtones of all these allusions must be candidly admitted. Since there are so many difficulties associated with the historicity of these Old Testament references, it is the poetry in the description, not the historicity of the event, which should be developed. As in all great poetry, something symbolic, something sacramental, points to a quite different reality. Baptismal water must be real water, but its sacramental quality resides in its symbolism. In this sense, baptismal water does indeed become a "metaphor." The deepest mysteries of human life, such as love, can only be discovered and expressed in human symbols. So, too, God is discovered and expressed only in symbolic ways.

5. THE BAPTISMAL FORMULA MUST MENTION THE THREE DIVINE PERSONS

The Council of Trent does not make any definition regarding this formula. However, in the history of the church there has been a consistency in the use of this trinitarian formula.

COMMENTS

1. The doctrine of the Trinity developed slowly in early church history. As a result, early on there appear to have been baptisms "in the name of Jesus." Over the centuries other variations can be found. Trinity and Christology are inseparably united, and the concern of church leadership on this matter is this: the words of baptism must indicate that a person being baptized, and the community celebrating the baptism, are doing this in the name of God/Jesus. Whenever the formula makes this connection of baptism to God/Jesus unclear, church leadership has become very uneasy.

2. Relationship to Christian spirituality. Both the person being baptized and the community celebrating baptism are surrounded in this ritual celebration by the total economy of salvation history: God as creator (the Father); God as revealer (the Word made flesh); God as self-giving (the Spirit of divine life itself) surround those in the baptismal process and make God's own life truly and really present in each and every one who takes part in that same baptismal process. When we unpack this mystery of God's presence in baptismal celebration, we are developing the spiritual depth of one's baptism.

6. BAPTISM IS NECESSARY FOR SALVATION

There has been a consistent teaching in the Christian church that the salvation of the world is related to the paschal mystery of Jesus.

COMMENTS

1. The core of this official and solemn teaching is found in the consistent Christian belief that the salvation of all men and women is somehow connected to the life, death and resurrection of Jesus. When one moves to describe this relationship in detail, however, one has moved away from an "official and solemn" teaching into the area of theological speculation.

2. This Christian claim that salvation is related to Jesus has today become the most questioned religious issue facing the Christian churches. Fundamentalism thrives on a literal interpretation of this claim: unless someone accepts Jesus as his or her Lord and savior, that person will never be saved. As a result, there is immense missionary activity by these fundamentalist groups of Christians who want to bring people into a right-relationship with Jesus. In the Roman Catholic Church today, one can also find at times a fundamentalist approach in which missionary activity is seen exclusively in this: make people Roman Catholic. For those who press this approach, any missionary activity which preaches the kingdom of God, not the Roman Catholic Church, is unacceptable. Only those missionary activities which preach the Roman Catholic Church as the one true church are valid missionary movements. Ecumenical discussion has refocused this question, presenting all the churches, including the Roman Catholic Church, with the issue: are "other" churches truly the church which Jesus instituted? Even the phrase, "salvation in Jesus," is not all that clear, since one immediately asks: which Jesus? The Lutheran Jesus? the Anglican Jesus? the Byzantine Jesus? the Roman Catholic Jesus? When one moves beyond the Christian framework into the ecumenical discussions with world religions, the question of the centrality of Jesus for salvation becomes even more acute. Are Buddhists not saved? Are Hindus not saved? Are Jews not saved? Are Islamic people not saved? As of right now, all theological explanations of this centrality of Jesus for salvation remain theological speculations, and religious education teachers are surely aware that there is no defined official "Roman Catholic" position as regards these theological views. Still, raising the many issues in a religion class can be of tremendous help to today's students who live within a multicultural and multireligious world. Even if no final answer is possible on this issue of religious freedom and religious pluralism, guidelines can be developed.

3. **Relationship to Christian spirituality.** Spiritual life is a journey, and for a Christian this spiritual journey is a quest for the meaning of God/Jesus. From this viewpoint, a Christian will always be in search of the full meaning of the incarnation. Were one to have a full understanding of the incarnation, the incarnation itself would cease to be a mystery. This means that Christian spirituality will always have a grey or unfinished side. At the core of Christian spirituality is, of course, the meaning of Jesus, and thus there will always be a grey or unfinished aspect of Jesus. In our spiritual journey, we are searching for the meaning of Jesus. We do not start our journey with full clarity; we do not travel in full clarity. Jesus is called the light of the world, but often that light only shows us the next

step or two. Helping students relate one's spiritual journey with Jesus and with an acceptance of many unfinished and unanswered questions is a major part of religious spiritual education.

7. BAPTISM IMPRINTS A CHARACTER ON THE SOUL

This is found in the Council of Trent, *Decree on the Sacraments,* can. 9, in which it is stated that baptism confers a character.

COMMENTS

1. That baptism confers a character is defined. What that character might be has not been defined. Any description of what that character is, therefore, remains a theological view, of which there are several. The major issue in this particular solemn teaching of the church is intrinsically connected to the non-repetition of baptism during one's earthly life. Once a person is baptized, baptism is never repeated. It is on the basis of this issue of not repeating baptism that any discussion of the church's official teaching on baptism should rest. When one goes beyond this base, theological opinions are at work.

2. Relationship to Christian spirituality. The baptismal relationship of character and spirituality follows the same pattern mentioned earlier in the section on the three sacramental characters.

8. THERE IS ONE BAPTISM FOR THE REMISSION OF SIN

In the many official creeds of the church we pray: "We believe . . . in one baptism for the remission of sin."

COMMENTS

1. Two things are at the core of this teaching: baptism is not based on persons or sects. One is not baptized into a local church or into a group under the leadership of some charismatic individual. One is baptized by the Lord himself into the church of God. Secondly, the core of this teaching is this: baptism is related to the remission of sin, and therefore with God's grace. Since only God remits sin and only God gives grace, in baptism we are ultimately face-to-face with God, not with something human.

2. In today's ecumenical framework, this "one baptism" means that the baptism in other Christian churches is accepted as true baptism. In Roman Catholicism, we do not "rebaptize" Lutherans, Anglicans, etc., who want to become Roman Catholics. However, this is not simply a church regulation: do not rebaptize. The acceptance of baptism, in whatever Christian denomination, raises many theological issues. The most pressing theological issue today on this matter involves the eucharist. If we as Roman Catholics accept the baptism of Eastern Catholics and of Protestants, and if baptism and eucharist are intrinsically united from a theological standpoint, on what basis can we deny a baptized Christian the reception of the eucharist? Several answers have been given, and the one which is most often heard is this: there is not yet a "full communion." However, this implies that there is not yet a "full" meaning of baptism, and yet if baptism is "one" how can it be divided into "less" and "full"? In the Vatican response to the Final Statement of Anglican/Roman Catholic dialogues, this "full communion" was emphatically placed on the acceptance/non-acceptance of the pope. However, this too raises many questions, since if we accept "one" baptism and therefore the baptism of those who do not accept the pope, what are we saying about this solemn teaching of "one" baptism? By the term, one baptism, and by our acceptance of the validity of baptism in other churches, we are saying that these non-Roman Catholic baptisms are sacramentally what baptism is all about even though there is no acceptance of the pope. This entire issue is clearly a major issue today, and religious education teachers cannot avoid controversial issues even if there are no conclusive solutions to the problems involved.

   3. Relationship to Christian spirituality. Spiritual life leads to a unitive life and the teaching on "one baptism" points us in this direction of mystical union as the goal of our spiritual journey. God is a uniting God, and all baptized Christians are drawn together by a uniting God in a uniting sacrament. Baptism is, therefore, social not private. It affects an individual person, but if the social and unifying dimension is not operative, baptism becomes distorted. Many students today are seeking spirituality which is social, not private, and a spirituality which leads to union not to disunion.

9. BAPTISM AND ORIGINAL SIN

   At the Council of Trent, the bishops issued a special *Decree on Original Sin.* In this decree, baptism is said to take away original sin.

COMMENTS

   1. The Council of Trent taught (a) that baptism does not simply cover over original sin, but takes it away; (b) that concupiscence is not to be identified with original sin. The bishops at Trent also taught that original sin is a situation in which all human beings share. They did not teach that because we are human we are sinful, but rather, sin, even original sin, is never simply a private matter. All sinfulness has a social dimension.

2. However, in Roman Catholic theology today, there are many divergent views on the exact meaning of original sin, all of which are acceptable. In other words, there is no clear defined teaching on the core meaning of original sin. Religious education teachers must be careful not to present a specific theological view as regards original sin as the "doctrine of the church." Assuredly, this does not make the catechesis on original sin easy for religious education teachers; indeed, this diverse theological spectrum makes such a catechesis even more difficult. Original sin is called a "sin" only in an analogous way. Even with this kind of analogous description, what original sin really is remains unclear. What is meant by analogy? What is meant by a state, rather than an action? What is meant when we hear that original sin is a sin contracted but not committed?

3. The historicity of Adam and Eve is very much in doubt. The Adam and Eve story in the book of Genesis is a wonderful religious story, but in today's scientific world view, the historical reality of an Adam and Eve cannot be maintained. Students will surely raise questions on this issue. Anthropological data does not move in the direction of an historical Adam and Eve. The account in Genesis should be seen as a Jewish way of looking at the origin of the world, just as other cultures have developed mythological accounts of the origin of the world. There is no definition by the Roman Catholic Church that Adam and Eve were truly historical figures and truly the first human beings.

4. Over the centuries, the theological teaching on original sin has continually emphasized that we are fragile human beings in everything we do, including our moral efforts. At the Council of Trent the bishops refused to accept a view of human nature which said that human nature was intrinsically corrupt and that baptismal grace merely covered over the basic corruption of men and women. At the Council of Trent, the Protestant position on grace and original sin was presented to the bishops in this fashion. The bishops, however, did not want to say that human beings, after original sin, are essentially evil. This view would lead to an understanding that God, after the fall, has created "evil beings." However, can an all-good God create something intrinsically evil? The bishops at Trent rejected such a view of God.

On the other hand, some earlier writers, such as Pelagius, had taught that a human person, independently of God, takes the first step to acquire grace. God's grace then becomes an "award" for something humanly good. St. Augustine developed his teaching on original sin to combat this "rosy" view of human nature with its denial that God's grace is absolutely free. Whenever Christian writers have made grace an "award" for some good work, these writers are following in the footsteps of Pelagius and have been time and again rejected by church leadership.

The teaching on original sin, however, has itself not always found a middle way between these two extremes, and at times the teaching became somewhat distorted. This is the reason why today many Roman Catholic theologians are attempting to rethink the very meaning of original sin, and this work is not yet completed. A religious education teacher is well-advised to walk carefully when discussing the issue of original sin and be honest with the students in admitting that the issues involved are not as yet resolved.

5. Relationship to Christian spirituality. There is a major value for one's spiritual life in the teaching on original sin, namely, that we are all morally fragile and weak. This does not mean we are intrinsically evil, but only that we are imperfect and cannot really move on in our spiritual life unless God reaches out *first* and helps us. Perhaps there is some helpful pedagogical connection between this human fragility and the twelve-step program for addiction. Only when someone says: "I am addicted," can health and growth begin. Only when we admit that we are spiritually fragile, does God's grace strengthen us. Theologically, however, a distinction must be made: even the admission of our human fragile nature comes from God's grace. No good work ever "causes" grace. Grace causes every good work.

The Sacrament of Holy Baptism
Teachings of the Ordinary Magisterium

There are two major sources for the baptismal teachings of the ordinary magisterium:

1. The baptismal rituals, namely: the *Rite of Christian Initiation of Adults (RCIA)*, the *Rite of Baptism for Children,* and the new *Rite of Baptism for Children of Catechetical Age.*

2. The section on baptism in the revised code of canon law.

The mere inclusion of something in a ritual, such as the *RCIA* ritual, or the mere inclusion of something in a code of canon law, does not give that teaching any defined status. Canon law does not by itself establish any defined doctrine. There are, of course, references to defined teachings in the code of canon law, but the reason for their status of "defined teaching" can never be based simply on their inclusion in a given canon. In other words, one cannot quote canon law as the basis for a solemn teaching of the church or a "last word" for defined church doctrine.

The same is true for the rituals. There are solemn and official truths expressed in these rituals, but the reason for their "official and solemn" status is not based on their inclusion in a *RCIA* or the two rituals for the baptism of children. One cannot quote a ritual as the basis for a solemn teaching of the church or a "last word" for defined church doctrine.

Nonetheless, this kind of documentation remains official; it is called the ordinary magisterium of the church. The significance this has for religious education is as follows: teachers will use these documents for their presentation of baptism, but students, however, should never get the idea that either the rituals or the code as such, are the "final word," or the "infallible teaching" of the church. Students should learn that these are serious and official teachings of the church, but later rituals and later codes will undoubtedly make substantial changes both in ritual and code. Wherever there is a question of some "defined" or "solemn and official" teaching of the church, teachers will make it crystal-clear that the status of such a teaching rests on something more fundamental than a ritual or a code, and the teachers will provide the students with such documentation.

It has happened too many times in our day and age that good Roman Catholics have remained fixed in something merely "canonical" or merely "ritualistic" as if these were the unchanging teachings of the church. One cannot blame these Roman Catholics, since too often this was precisely the way they were taught. Nor can one blame the religious education teachers of former times, because this, too, was the way they were taught. In the framework of religious education prior to Vatican II and even during the council itself, it was the seminary system which provided the future priests with religious and theological education. After ordination, these priests then went on to teach the religious educators, who then went on to teach the children and the teenagers. Unfortunately, the seminary training itself did not adequately teach the seminarians how to distinguish the changeable doctrines from the unchangeable doctrines. Many priests who were educated in that era felt that canon law provided the limits beyond which one should never go. They felt that rituals were to be followed minutely. When they did this, the doctrine of the Roman Catholic Church, in their understanding, was being preserved in a correct manner, indeed the only correct manner. In today's religious education, we cannot make the same kind of mistake. Catechesis must seriously present the unchanging teaching and also seriously present the changing teaching. All of this is happening today and there is a much more careful weighing of the changeable and the unchangeable.

The Sacrament of Holy Baptism
Unresolved Issues

The following are some of the more important issues regarding baptism that have as yet attained neither theological nor doctrinal resolution.

1. A CLEARER UNDERSTANDING OF THE NECESSITY OF BAPTISM FOR SALVATION

The *Catechism of the Catholic Church,* in its brief overview of the necessity of baptism, repeats a position expressed by many theologians: "God has linked salvation to the sacrament of baptism, but God is not bound to sacraments" [1257]. That God is not bound to a sacrament is further emphasized in 1260: "We are obliged to hold that the Holy Spirit offers everyone the possibility of sharing in this paschal mystery in a manner known to God." These sentences echo sections of the documents of Vatican II. Those who are unbaptized can be saved. God offers grace to all.

In today's multicultural and multireligious world the "necessity of baptism" remains, however, an unresolved issue. For instance, when the question of baptism and Christian evangelization is connected to the issue of religious freedom, which Vatican II affirmed, serious questions about the meaning of Roman Catholic missionary activity begin to arise. Religious education teachers will surely be confronted by numerous questions from students on the issues of evangelization, missionary activity, and religious freedom.

2. A CLEARER UNDERSTANDING OF THE RELATIONSHIP BETWEEN BAPTISM AND ORIGINAL SIN

The theology of baptism which was prevalent prior to Vatican II was strongly controlled by the teaching of original sin. This is not the case today. Even in the *Ritual of Baptism for Children,* original sin is mentioned only once. In the baptismal section of the *Catechism of the Catholic Church,* original sin is mentioned, but not in a controlling way. The new code of canon law states that baptism of a baby should be done within the first weeks after birth. The former canon stated that baptism of an infant should take place *quam primum* after birth [as soon as possible]. The new canon [867] uses the term *quam primum* for the parents; the parents are to begin arrangements for baptism *quam primum.* In this subtle change in the canons, one also notes a movement away from a baptismal theology, controlled by original sin. What does all this say to the religious education teacher? The precise meaning of original sin and its relationship to baptism remains, in today's church, an unresolved issue.

3. BAPTISM: A REMEDY FOR SIN OR A CELEBRATION OF GRACE?

Is the sacrament of baptism a remedy for sin or is it a celebration of God's free gift of grace? Books on baptism will still state that baptism takes away all sin, original and personal. Baptism will take away as well all penalties for sin. On the other hand, these same books will emphasize that baptism makes one a new creation. Currently, sacramental emphasis falls on the positive aspect. In baptism, we celebrate primarily God's action, God's loving presence. We celebrate primarily God's free gift of grace. In a classroom presentation, instead of saying: "In baptism, not only sin is forgiven, but also grace is given"; the following emphasis would be better: "Not only does God freely give us grace but God also makes us a new creature. Being a new creature means that God has freely forgiven our sins." Does one start with grace? Or, does one start with sin? Are the sacraments primarily remedies of sin (the medieval and tridentine view), or are sacraments primarily celebrations of God's love (the more current theological view)?

4. BAPTISM AND THE EQUALITY OF ALL CHRISTIANS

In baptism, all the human limitations of nation, culture, race and sex are transcended. However, there remains even in the church, and not just in society, a certain "racism," i.e., a preference for one culture or racial approach over another, and there remains a certain "sexism," i.e., women in the church are not equal to men. There is a clear clash between the baptismal equality on the one hand and the actual form of church life on the other. This is a major unresolved issue of this present age.

5. ONE BAPTISM AND THE ECUMENICAL MOVEMENT

There is one baptism, which establishes a sacramental bond of unity among those reborn by it. All who have been baptized or, as some writers prefer to express it, who have been justified by faith through baptism, are incorporated into Christ, are called Christians, and become brothers and sisters in the Lord. If this is true baptismal theology and teaching—which it surely is—why are baptized non-Roman Catholics unable to receive communion with us? Protestants can, of course, do so on special occasions, and with the Eastern churches there is a full eucharistic openness, whenever spiritual need arises. The usual theological claim that the non-Roman Catholic baptized Christians are not "fully" united to the true church raises serious baptismal questions: Is their baptism not "fully" baptism? Is baptism only a "preliminary step" to real Christian status? Even official documents of the church, such as the Vatican response to the final report of the Anglican/Roman Catholic dialogues, have only complicated these questions by raising the issue of the papacy in a major way. Almost half of the official response focuses on the Anglicans' rejection of the papacy, with the consequence that Anglicans are not fully united to the Catholic faith. Yet the question immediately arises: If one does not accept the papacy, is one's baptism incomplete? Once again, there are unresolved and complicated issues of enormous consequence, which cannot be ignored.

6. THE THEOLOGICAL UNDERSTANDING OF BAPTISMAL CHARACTER

The doctrine on baptismal character has only one immutable issue: baptism is never repeated. When teachers or writers begin to speak of configuration, sealing with an indelible mark, a mark of consecration, a pledge of Christian service, etc., one is deep within the area of theological views, and competing theological views as well. On the issue of what baptismal character might truly be, no resolution appears to be even remotely on the horizon.

4

The Sacrament of Holy Confirmation

Most religious educators today find the preparation for the sacrament of confirmation one of the more difficult parts of their catechesis. So much of the material on confirmation is unclear and unfocused. Religious education teachers will, however, find some details of major importance which will provide help as they prepare young people for the sacrament of confirmation.

First of all, there is in much of the written material a continued stress on the unity of the three sacraments: baptism, confirmation, and eucharist. Such an intrinsic unity should also become a major stress in any religious education presentation of confirmation. Second, the issue of age remains a constant theme as regards confirmation, but there appears to be an increasing effort to move away from the age issue as the most dominant consideration. Third, almost all the written material emphasizes in a more detailed way the role of the Holy Spirit in confirmation. This emphasis on the Spirit is key to any solid educational presentation of confirmation.

Religious education teachers will find that the four foundational ideas for all sacraments, mentioned above, might well serve a presentation on confirmation, namely:

1. The primacy of God's action
   The sacrament of confirmation is primarily a sacrament celebrating what God does, not what we do.

2. The centrality of Christ
   The sacrament of confirmation, as every church liturgy, primarily celebrates the paschal mystery by which Christ has saved us.

3. The Spirit of Jesus
   The sacrament of confirmation focuses on the role of the Spirit of Jesus in the life of a confirmed Christian.

4. The community called church
   The sacrament of confirmation is a celebration by the total community, *Christus totus.*

From an historical standpoint, one can say that in the Western church, and only in the Western church, from the eleventh century onward, and *only* from the eleventh century onward, does one find a separated celebration of confirmation as the general practice. Because of this late appearance of confirmation as a sacrament separate from baptism, the tracing of "confirmation in the economy of salvation" is really impossible. The economy of salvation has left many written testimonies about the presence of the Holy Spirit in the life of the Jewish people and in the early Christian communities, but to conclude that these references refer to a sacrament of confirmation is impossible. Nor can one say that during the patristic period there was in the West a "double sacrament," while in the East the two sacraments were celebrated in one liturgical rite. All of this indicates that an historical problem exists: namely, up to the eleventh century, can one even speak about two "sacraments" in any secure and grounded way? If one does attempt to find in historical material prior to 1000 indications of confirmation, how solid is the evidence and how widespread is it? Religious education teachers have access today to several well-crafted books on the history of the sacrament of confirmation. Using such books, they are able to present a clear historical framework for the catechesis on this sacrament.

Confirmation in the Roman Catholic Church is a sacramental rite. This cannot be said of "confirmation" in the Anglican and Protestant churches. These churches do not consider confirmation a sacrament, even though they have a ritual called "confirmation." In the non-uniate Eastern churches, confirmation is again not considered a sacrament in the Roman Catholic understanding of this term, namely, as a sacrament separate from baptism. Consequently, religious education teachers must be very careful in making comparisons of Roman Catholic confirmation with non-Roman Catholic rituals, even if these latter rituals are called "confirmation."

In addressing a "theology of confirmation," authors often use a manner of speaking which has some validity, but which at the same time is confusing. This involves statements which speak of confirmation in the framework of "more." For example, one has read or heard something like the following expressions:

> In confirmation, the baptized are linked *more perfectly* to the church.

> Those confirmed are *more strictly* obliged to spread and defend the faith.

> In confirmation the gift of the Spirit *increases* the grace of baptism.

> Through confirmation, Christians share *more completely* in the mission of Jesus.

> The character of confirmation is a sign of our *total* belonging to Jesus.

> Confirmation is a *completion* of baptism.

In all of these statements—and many others might be cited—we hear such words as:

> more, complete, perfect, increase, total.

Such words imply, however, that prior to confirmation, the situation was:

> less, not complete, less perfect, less full, not total.

There is a validity to this kind of religious and theological language, since every prayer, each response to God's grace, every act of compassion, and every sacrament "increases," "fulfills," "perfects," etc., our Christian life. This increasing and perfecting happens both in sacramental actions and outside of sacramental actions. When this is used specifically of a sacramental action, such as confirmation, and the comparison is made to a sacramental situation prior to confirmation, the comparison of "more" implies an "incompleteness" of baptism, or in the case of those who have received both baptism and eucharist, an "incompleteness" of both baptism and eucharist. The theological issue arises in a very austere way when one attempts to explain the incompleteness of baptism and eucharist. This issue raises fundamental questions about the "completing" or "fulfilling" or "perfecting" status of confirmation.

Confirmation	Baptism/Eucharist
Bound more perfectly to the church	Bound less perfectly to the church
Fullness of the Holy Spirit	Less filled by the Holy Spirit
Sharing more completely in Christ's mission	Sharing less completely in Christ's mission
The Holy Spirit marks our total beginning	The Holy Spirit marks a partial beginning
United more firmly to Christ	United less firmly to Christ
Grants a special strength to spread and defend the faith	Does not grant this special strength to spread and defend the faith
Completes baptism	Baptism is incomplete
Perfects the common priesthood of the faithful	Less perfect belonging to the common priesthood

This kind of language is not wrong, but as the outline above indicates, it is ambiguous. When one makes such "more" statements about confirmation, then one must go to great lengths to explain the "less" implication for baptism/eucharist. Whether one considers an infant, a child of catechetical age or a teenager, who has just received confirmation, it is pedagogically and theologically unclear how we can call such a person more perfectly bound to the church; sharing more completely in Christ's mission; more firmly united to the Holy Spirit; a more perfect priest in the priesthood of all believers. Confirmation does not make people "super Christians," and our language describing confirmation should not foster such a view.

Since there is today such widespread theological and liturgical ambiguity about confirmation, one would expect that the language about confirmation will also be ambiguous. Needless to say, it is.

Are there, teachers might ask, any "immutable" teachings on confirmation which should appear in the catechesis on confirmation? The answer is yes, but they are very few. The following is a list of the "defined" teachings of the church on this sacrament, although as part of a curriculum, such a list would never be a unit all by itself.

The Sacrament of Holy Confirmation Defined Teaching

1. CONFIRMATION IS A SACRAMENT

This is found in the Council of Trent, *Decree on the Sacraments,* sacraments in general, can. 1, which lists all seven sacraments.

COMMENTS

1. From the eleventh century onward in the West, confirmation came to be considered as one of the official sacraments of the church. The definition of Trent, made in the sixteenth century, states that confirmation is one of the seven sacraments. No definition was made about its history. No definition was made as to the "time" when it was instituted. The core focus was simply on the sacramentality of confirmation.

2. A major reason for this stance by the bishops at Trent was this: At the time of Trent, the historical data on confirmation was beginning to emerge, with the result that Calvin and Luther, as well as others, called confirmation an invention by bishops. The bishops at Trent reacted, to some degree, in the way described in the caveat, mentioned earlier in this book: namely, the focus in their arguments on many occasions moved away from the sacramental issue to the issue of the bishops' authority in matters sacramental.

3. Relationship to Christian spirituality. The church, in calling confirmation a sacrament, emphasizes a major spiritual reality: God is acting in and through created things and people. We are urged to look beyond the aspects of ritual: the oil and its blessing; the laying on of hands; the prayers and ceremonies. We are urged to see through them and in them God's compassion for us, God's own real presence in the celebration of confirmation. Even our emphasis on the term "Holy Spirit" should not move us from this search, for the Holy Spirit is God, and it is the real presence of God in me and in us that we are celebrating in confirmation.

2. THE BISHOP IS THE ORDINARY MINISTER OF CONFIRMATION

This is found in the Council of Trent, *Decree on the Sacraments,* can. 3 on confirmation: "If anyone says that the ordinary minister of the holy confirmation is not the bishop alone, but any simple priest, let that person be anathema."

COMMENTS

1. The focus of this definition is on one issue only: the bishop is the ordinary minister of confirmation. No clarification of "ordinary" is provided by the bishops of the council. As a result, there is some unclarity with the meaning of this canon: namely, how one should understand the term "ordinary."

2. In the *Catechism of the Catholic Church,* the authors use a different term: the "originating minister" is the bishop. This is the term which was used by the bishops at Vatican II (*Lumen Gentium* 26). In the current *RCIA* and the *Rite of Baptism for Children of Catechetical Age,* the priest who administers confirmation is the same person who administers baptism. Neither of these rituals indicates that such a minister is, in these circumstances, an extraordinary minister of confirmation. Quite the contrary. In both rituals the priest who administers both baptism and confirmation is the ordinary minister of these sacraments. Since data on a sacrament of confirmation separated from baptism, prior to the eleventh century, is difficult to establish, one can hardly use patristic sources to indicate that the *episkopos* of that early time was the "originating" or "ordinary" minister of confirmation. At that time, confirmation as a sacrament separate from baptism is extremely hard to document. As a result, even speaking about "confirmation" in the patristic period is a very complex and elusive theme, and finding references to a minister of confirmation is much more complex and illusive.

3. Relationship to Christian spirituality. Bishops signify both the local, diocesan church and the relationship of the local church to the wider church. Confirmation has a spiritual side, which precisely reflects this same dual-symbol. Confirmation is a sacrament which indicates that we are members of a local community called church, but it also indicates that we are members of the wider church, the people of God. These people of God are in every race and in every land throughout the world; these people of God are both male and female. Confirmation opens one to the unending or unlimited compassion of God, a compassion that includes myself but includes others as well, and these others go far beyond my own small world. The spirituality of confirmation is an unselfish spirituality, urging one to mirror this compassionate God and to show love to all equally. Rather than a confirmation spirituality, which speaks in terms of soldier of Christ and fighting for the faith, confirmation spirituality is a spirituality which turns swords into plowshares. As the bishop represents both the local and the wider church, those who are confirmed are Spirit-urged men and women who bring the compassion of God to the local church and to the wider church, regardless of race, regardless of gender, regardless of position.

3. CONFIRMATION CONFERS A CHARACTER

This is found in the Council of Trent, *Decree on the Sacraments,* can. 9, which states that the three sacraments confer a character.

COMMENTS

1. The only "defined" issue in this teaching is that confirmation confers a character. There is no definition as to what this character is. The focus of the character is this: confirmation is not to be repeated.

2. The only reason why confirmation is said to confer a character and the only reason, therefore, why confirmation can only be celebrated once in a lifetime is the relationship which confirmation has with baptism. If confirmation were totally separate from baptism, it is quite conceivable that it could be a sacrament that one might receive several times during one's lifetime. This connection to baptism limits the way in which a Roman Catholic theologian or religious education teacher can speak about confirmation, and it limits the way in which a Roman Catholic liturgist can plan a celebration of confirmation.

3. Relationship to Christian spirituality. The relationship of the confirmation/character teaching to spirituality is the same as that of baptism. Other metaphors might be used, e.g., soldier of Christ or adult profession of faith, but these metaphors are only theological opinions and therefore cannot be taught as though they were the official approach of the church to confirmation.

The Sacrament of Holy Confirmation
Teachings of the Ordinary Magisterium

Much of the material on the ordinary magisterium of the church as regards sacraments in general or baptism applies to the sacrament of confirmation. Diocesan regulations on confirmation continue to be diverse, since most of these regulations are controlled by the issue of age. On the issue of age, the revised canon law favors an early age. More often than not, diocesan regulations favor a later age. In the *Rite of Baptism for Children of Catechetical Age,* the baptizing minister should confirm. Pastors do not have the licit power to change this part of the ritual and forbid such confirmations. However, as is well known, this early confirming then produces two sets of students in a religious education program: those who will eventually prepare for confirmation with many hours of preparation and, in the same classroom, those who have already received confirmation, with no such length of preparation.

The Sacrament of Holy Confirmation
Unresolved Issues

There are a number of unresolved issues, and as a result every religious education teacher will find it more than difficult to synthesize and interrelate all aspects of this sacrament. The major unresolved issues include:

1. THE AGE FOR CONFIRMATION

The issue of age for confirmation dominates almost all discussions on the sacrament of confirmation. Diocesan regulations, for the most part, are controlled by a decision regarding a certain age for confirmation. Parish discussions fare no better. When one moves beyond the North American church, one finds that confirmation is not administered at the same age-level which we in the United States find customary. When one moves to the Eastern churches, an entirely different understanding of confirmation appears, for which age is not the controlling factor.

2. THE RELATIONSHIP BETWEEN CONFIRMATION AND BAPTISM

The issue of confirmation's relationship to baptism remains unclear in theological material. Is confirmation a totally different sacrament than baptism? Is it essentially connected to baptism? Is confirmation merely a reaffirmation of one's baptism? From a theological and historical standpoint, the more that confirmation is separated from baptism the more unclear it becomes. From a pastoral standpoint, at least in the Anglo-European world, the more that confirmation is separated from baptism the clearer it seems to become.

3. THE HISTORY OF CONFIRMATION WITH ITS PROBLEMS

The history of the sacrament of confirmation calls into question many elements that have been called "traditional." Even the theological view of a development of doctrine does not assuage the problems. The claims for a sacrament of confirmation in historical data predating the year 1000 are continually challenged by serious scholarship. All of this discussion on the history of the sacrament of confirmation has repercussions on the issue of "seven sacraments." Religious education teachers will not find, to date, any clear resolution of these issues.

4. THE SEQUENCING OF THE SACRAMENTS

From a pastoral point of view, the issue of the progression of the sacramental rituals, namely, baptism, confirmation, eucharist on the one hand, or baptism [reconciliation], eucharist, confirmation on the other, presents a religious education teacher with enormous hurdles. When one attempts to bring elements of developmental education into the issue of sacramental sequencing, a teacher is confronted with the ordinary magisterium of the church which prescribes a certain sequencing, even though there has been serious criticism by teachers. This issue will not go away by any "fiat" from church authority. Developmental educational issues must be taken seriously by all parties concerned, teachers and church leadership. The new *Rite of Baptism for Children of Catechetical Age* only complicates the situation, since religious education teachers will find in their classes students already confirmed and students who need preparation for confirmation.

5. CONFIRMATION AND THE ECUMENICAL DIALOGUES

The ecumenical issues regarding confirmation have not merited much dialogue. The positions of the Roman Catholic Church and of the non-uniate Eastern churches are very polar. The positions of the Roman Catholic Church and of the Anglican Church and of various Protestant churches are even more diverse. However, the sacrament of confirmation, by itself, is not central to the ecumenical dialogue, and, as a result, this theme is not discussed in any profound way.

6. THE NECESSITY OF CONFIRMATION

The necessity of the sacrament of confirmation has never been adequately established, once a ritual, separate from baptism, began to emerge in the Western church. In the revised code of canon law we read: "The faithful are obliged to receive this sacrament at the appropriate time" (canon 890). In the earlier version of canon law, it was stated that confirmation was not necessary as a means of salvation, but no one should neglect receiving it, if the opportunity to do so arose (canon 787). In 1946 the Sacred Congregation for the Discipline of the Sacraments stated that confirmation was not required for the salvation of one's soul as a necessary means (*de necessitate medii*). When church leadership uses such ambivalent descriptions of the necessity of this sacrament, a religious education teacher can only find it difficult to convince both young people and parents that the reception of this sacrament is really a necessary part of our Roman Catholic life.

7. THE RELATIONSHIP BETWEEN CONFIRMATION AND THE CHURCH AS A BASIC SACRAMENT

The relationship of confirmation as a sacrament to the church as a basic sacrament, and to Jesus as the primordial sacrament, generally receives only the smallest attention by theologians. Since theologians have not written in any detailed way on this relationship, a religious education teacher will be at a loss to find adequate background material.

Central to all these unresolved issues are two different stances. Each position has its own set of theologians, liturgists, religious education teachers, parents, bishops and even Vatican congregations. The first stance, urged on by biblical and historical data, moves in the direction of uniting baptism and confirmation as closely as possible, even making them one sacrament. The other stance, urged on by very legitimate pastoral needs, moves in the direction of making confirmation a significant stage in one's spiritual journey, quite distinct from baptism, first eucharist, and first reconciliation, which are also significant stages of one's spiritual journey. Because of the polarity behind each of these two stances, most discussions on confirmation, at a school, parish, diocesan, or episcopal conference level, end up in ambiguity.

Even with these two polar positions, most of the debated and unresolved issues are not really focused on the sacrament of confirmation itself, but on the religious presuppositions and the life experiences which one brings to these debates. Presuppositions about the meaning of church, about human experience, about religion, about self-identity, etc., are at work. As such, the rule of thumb, indicated above, would be quite valid here: refocus the discussion not on confirmation, but on the presuppositions.

5

The Sacrament of Holy Eucharist

Every classroom discussion on eucharist should emphasize the unity of baptism, confirmation, and eucharist, since eucharist is an integral part of Christian initiation. This unity of the three sacramental actions is fairly consistent in current theological discussion, but religious education teachers will have to find creative ways to make their presentation of eucharist unified within a baptismal/confirmational/eucharistic framework.

Pedagogically, one might help integrate the presentation on the eucharist with baptism and confirmation by stressing once again the foundational ideas of all liturgical action: namely

1. that liturgy, and especially eucharistic liturgy, is above all a celebration of the action of God, not a celebration of human action;

2. that eucharistic liturgy celebrates primarily the paschal mystery of Jesus;

3. that eucharistic liturgy is the action of the Holy Spirit;

4. and finally that eucharistic liturgy is fundamentally a celebration of the entire Christian community, the *Christus totus.*

With these four centralizing issues in mind, let us consider first of all some current issues on eucharistic theology, which the documents of Vatican II and other post-conciliar documents have presented to the Christian community.

1. THE EUCHARIST AS SUMMIT AND SOURCE OF CHURCH LIFE

There is a passage from the documents of Vatican II which states that the eucharist is the "summit and source of the church's life." [*Lumen Gentium,* 11] Other similar passages from the documents of Vatican II have also been cited both by theologians and by official documents. Religious education teachers know that some additional explanation of this statement is necessary, at least for the upper grades of religious catechesis. In the lives of most Catholics, students will say, the eucharist generally means about one hour weekly on a late Saturday afternoon or on Sunday. How can this brief time be considered the "source" and the "summit" of one's entire Christian life? How can one answer such a question?

Religious educators hope to instill in students a form of life in which Christian principles are operative far more frequently than merely during one hour of the week. Religious educators know that the more one stresses the one-hour-weekly eucharist as the "source and summit" of Catholic life, the less Catholic the remainder of one's life might easily become. The source and summit should be a daily operative source and summit, not simply a weekly one. Teachers will have to spend time on this idea of the eucharist as the "summit and source" of church life, carefully explaining the very meaning of such a phrase. Perhaps the following material will be of some help.

The New Testament contains many passages about love as the summit and source of Christian discipleship: love of one's neighbor, love of one's enemy, and love of one's self, all of which move a person to love God. In Matthew, there is the passage in which people are welcomed into the heavenly kingdom precisely on the basis of Christian love: When I was hungry, thirsty, naked, sick, or in prison, you helped me. Matthew does not say that people are welcomed into the kingdom of heaven because they attended the eucharist on Sundays. Students in the upper grades will surely point out this discrepancy. According to Matthew, is not love the summit and source of church life?

The gospels also tell us that the first and most important commandment is to love God with all our heart and soul, and the second most important commandment is to love our neighbor as we love ourselves. These two commandments indicate again that the source and summit of Christian life is not eucharist but love. On many occasions, the New Testament states that this loving attitude and behavior is the source and summit of Christian life. Upper-grade students will quickly point this out. How can a teacher respond?

Perhaps the threefold description of the ministry of Jesus, which Vatican II used throughout its documentation, provides some help in this matter: namely, *prophet, priest and king,* or less triumphantly described, *teacher, sanctifier and leader.* This order, in which prophet is placed first, is the more common in Vatican II documents, although in a few rare occasions the title, priest, is named first. Still, teaching and preaching the kingdom of God was the major mission and ministry of Jesus himself, and therefore the major mission and ministry of his followers. One is a preacher/teacher—a prophet—by parental teaching, by actual classroom teaching and by one's daily example of Christian living. When the title, prophet, is placed first among the three aspects of Jesus' mission and ministry, then the summit and source of Christian life is one's daily efforts to reflect Jesus and thereby proclaim Jesus. To teach as Jesus did is the "source" and "summit" of church life. This would indicate that our teaching should focus on love as the "source" and "summit" of Christian life.

Only when one focuses on the second title, "priestly aspect" of the threefold Christian mission and ministry, is the eucharist theologically described as the summit and source of the church's life. This means that only when one is considering the liturgical and sacramental life of the church, can one describe the eucharist as the "summit and source of the church's life." The context of *Lumen Gentium,* paragraph 11, in which the eucharist is called the "source and summit" of church life, is just such a lengthy description of the sacramental life of the church, enumerating sacrament after sacrament.

In the same document, *Lumen Gentium,* chapter 5, speaks of the call to holiness.

> All Christians in any state or walk of life are called to the fullness
> of Christian life and to the perfection of love, and by this holiness
> a more human manner of life is fostered also in earthly society.

Throughout this entire chapter, holiness is called the "fullness of the Christian life," the "perfection" of Christian life. In paragraph 41 the document describes the goal of Christian holiness in the lives of bishops, priests, deacons, other ministers, married couples, widows, single people, those who work, the poor, the sick, the suffering. No Christian is left out of this list, and throughout this lengthy description eucharist is hardly mentioned. Rather, as it states clearly in paragraph 42:

> "God is love, and he who abides in love abides in God and God
> abides in him" [1 Jn. 4:16]. God has poured out his love in our
> hearts through the Holy Spirit, who has been given to us [cf.

Rom. 5:5]; therefore *the first and most necessary gift is charity,* by which we love God above all things and our neighbor because of him.

Love, or charity, is called the "first and most necessary gift." Would not love or charity be, then, the "source and summit" of Christian life? To reach the fullness and perfection of Christian life (summit), and to draw deeply from the grace of God's love (source), one "must frequently partake of the sacraments, chiefly the eucharist" [42]. The eucharist, in this paragraph, is presented as *an important means* to holiness, but not as the summit and source of Christian holiness. In this section of *Lumen Gentium,* the bishops present a very different view of the summit and source of the church's life.

Every religious educator will realize that the phrase, the eucharist is the "source and summit of the church's life," is not a phrase which is self-evident. In order to be clear, the phrase needs to be placed in a correct context. When we use the threefold description of Jesus' ministry, of the church's ministry, and of specific ordained and non-ordained ministries, namely, "prophet, priest, and king" [teacher, sanctifier, and leader], the eucharist as "source and summit of the church's life" makes more sense when such a teaching is connected not to prophet/teacher or to king/leader, but to priest/sanctifier. This means that the phrase has a limited and quite relative context. Only in a relative way can the eucharist be called a "summit and source of the church's life."

2. THE HISTORY OF EUCHARISTIC LITURGY AND EUCHARISTIC THEOLOGY

There have been several historical names for this central Christian ritual: *eucharist* is the most common name today within the Roman Catholic Church. Other names include: *the lord's supper,* the *breaking of the bread,* the *memorial of Jesus' passion and resurrection,* the *sacrifice of the mass,* and, in the Eastern churches, the *Divine Liturgy.* No single name can ever express fully the eucharistic mystery; each of these names has its own validity but each has its own limitations as well.

Along with this history of names for the eucharist, religious education teachers have at their disposal many carefully documented histories of the eucharist which present the biblical material in a quite scholarly way and which distinguish among the historical data those issues which can be clearly substantiated from those issues which are only conjectural. Historical material on the eucharist is extremely important, since in using it teachers are better equipped to indicate what is "immutable" and what is "changeable." In presenting the history of the eucharist, teachers should keep in mind the important statement of the *Catechism of the Catholic Church:* namely, *all lawfully recognized rites are of equal right and dignity* [1203]. The Roman Rite is simply one of these liturgies of equal right and equal dignity. The Roman Rite is not the norm against which all other liturgies are to be evaluated. Not even the Tridentine mass can be such a norm. The Roman Rite and one of its forms, the Tridentine mass, are but two eucharistic rituals alongside other equally valid and equally correct eucharistic rituals.

3. THE REAL PRESENCE OF JESUS

The word, "presence," and the mystery of Jesus' presence are the center of eucharistic theology and liturgy. According to Vatican II and also the encyclical of Paul VI, *Mysterium fidei,* Jesus is present when the church gathers together in prayer, when the church preaches or proclaims the word, and in the eucharistic prayer followed by holy communion. Most contemporary books on the eucharist mention these various occasions, in which Jesus is *really present* to the Christian community. Theologically, this is a new approach to "real presence," since in the past the term, "real presence," had been almost exclusively used for the eucharistic bread and wine. Students will read about this wider approach to real presence, and questions cannot help but arise. Is there a difference between Jesus' real presence in the gospel and the real presence in the form of bread and wine? Is Jesus more present in one way than in another way? For their part, teachers should realize that the theological integration of these various "real presences" is still being discussed and debated. No theological resolution has as yet been reached. All of these forms of presence are described by both the Vatican II documents and the encyclical of Paul VI as "real presence." Therefore, one should say quite clearly, that in the liturgical celebration of eucharist: Jesus is *really present* in the gathered community; Jesus is *really present* in the proclamation of the word; and Jesus is *really present* in the blessed bread and wine. In his encyclical, Paul VI states that in the eucharist Jesus is present *par excellence,* since this presence is "substantial." This explanation, based on the word, "substantial," is, however, only one of several theological views, which today attempt to clarify "why" eucharistic presence is a *par excellence* presence when compared to the real presence of Jesus elsewhere. The mere use of the term, substantial, really does not settle the matter in a satisfactory way. Scholastic theologians from the twelfth century onward, and the bishops at the Council of Trent used the term, substantial, to state that Jesus is not simply present in the eucharist in some "spiritual" way, through some memento or reminder or in a merely symbolic way. For them, the term, substantial, meant that Jesus himself, the one who sits at the right hand of the Father, was truly present. But this is the very way Jesus is also present in a gathered community of Christians, in the proclamation of the word, etc. In all of these situations, Jesus is present, not through some memento or reminder or in a merely symbolic way. The two terms, real and substantial, are not that clearly differentiated, and certainly not differentiated in any officially defined way. To date, there is no official teaching by the leadership of the Roman Catholic Church on this matter, precisely because this wider approach to the real presence is something quite new to Roman Catholic theology. Consequently, theologians are still struggling to find a way to bring all these "real presences" into some sort of clarity. Religious education teachers will, therefore, not have any "pat answers" to this issue.

4. THE CORE AND SUMMIT OF EUCHARISTIC CELEBRATION

In the *Catechism of the Catholic Church,* one reads in paragraph 1352 a major statement on eucharistic liturgy:

> The *Eucharistic Prayer* (*Anaphora*): With this prayer of thanksgiving and consecration, we come to the core and summit of the celebration.

Religious education teachers should make note of this statement. What is said here is key to an understanding of eucharist. In the eucharistic prayer, the *anaphora,* we have the *core or summit* of the eucharist. Too often, emphasis is so heavily placed on the reception of holy communion, that holy communion begins to be seen as the *core and summit* of the eucharist. Holy communion is indeed important, but it is of secondary importance. Holy communion is our response to the central eucharistic action. It is God's action which is the core and summit of the eucharistic celebration. It is God's action which brings Jesus really present to us. It is God's action which is the core and summit of our liturgical celebration. Holy communion is a very important but a secondary response by Christians to this primary action of God. This idea deserves all the emphasis it can get, and religious education teachers can unite this idea of the core and summit of eucharistic celebration to the four key ideas on all liturgical celebration to which I have persistently referred throughout this volume.

5. THE NOTION OF SACRIFICE AND THE EUCHARIST

Let us turn now to another key issue of eucharistic theology, namely, the issue of "sacrifice." As all religious education teachers know, the issue of the "sacrifice of the mass" became one of the major divisive issues during the Protestant Reformation and even today this issue remains a divisive one. Some historical background on the core questions regarding the sacrifice of the mass which were disputed at the time of the Reformation, and on the core issues which the bishops at Trent presented as the defined teaching of the church, is necessary to understand this truth of our faith.

In the *Decree on Justification* and in the *Doctrine on the Most Holy Sacrifice of the Mass,* the bishops at the Council of Trent clearly stated as part of Roman Catholic defined doctrine two basic positions:

1. the absolute gratuity of God's grace;

2. the full and adequate efficacy of Jesus' sacrifice.

Roman Catholics need to realize that when the bishops at Trent presented these two statements as defined doctrine, the position of the Roman Catholic Church and the position of the Lutheran and Calvinistic churches came into doctrinal agreement. The *Decree on Justification,* however, was promulgated by the Roman Catholic bishops after the split among the churches had taken place, and for a host of reasons there was no possibility of a reunion of the Christian community at that time.

Let us consider the grace issue first. If God's grace is absolutely gratuitous, then *we can do nothing to merit it.* Grace is a free gift of God's own self to us. When this is applied to sacramental theology, and in a special way to the eucharist, then great care must be taken by all teachers in the church—by the bishops, by the pre-school teachers, by other teachers, and by parents—to preserve in the eucharist the absolute gratuity of God's grace. What we do in the sacraments is only relatively important. In every sacramental action, what we do is always a response to what God in the sacrament has first done to and for us. Our actions are always response-actions. The Greek word, *eucharistia,* means precisely this: *thank you.* Every Sunday, the Catholic community assembles together to say to God: thank you. When we realize how much God has done for us, our response should surely be: *thank you.* Teachers are most correct when, in their presentation of eucharist, they lead the students again and again to a vision of what God has first done, is doing, and will continue to do in their lives. They will present the eucharist as a major moment in Catholic life when God, in Jesus, comes to the gathered community and, as a result, the community and the individual within that community celebrate in gratitude what God has first done. Sacraments can never be seen as a "manipulation" of God. God and God's grace do not depend on us. God's grace is a freely given gift. Great care must be taken by teachers so that the students never get the mechanical idea that when we say the correct words, Jesus is present. When we are good and receive holy communion, God will reward us. In this kind of statement, God's grace is made dependent on our human actions.

Second, the "sacrifice of Jesus" is fully efficacious by itself. Christians do not add to or complete this sacrifice. The church itself does not add to or complete this sacrifice. All language which implies that individual Christians or the church itself "completes" the once and for all efficacious sacrifice of Jesus is contrary to defined doctrine. In other words, teachers cannot present the sacrifice of Jesus as only 99% effective, awaiting our 1% in order to be fully effective. We do not "complete the sufferings of Jesus," as though the sufferings of Jesus were wanting. Many writers are at times too ambiguous when they speak about the "sacrifice of the church" or the "sacrifice of the people of God." Not enough care is taken by such authors to relate this "sacrifice of the church" idea to the official and solemnly defined teaching of the church that the sacrifice of Jesus is full and adequate by itself. We do not "save ourselves." Salvation is a gift, a grace, and this gift of salvation has been given to us through Jesus.

How a celebration of the eucharist is a representation of the one totally efficacious sacrifice of Jesus remains part of ongoing theological discussion. The bishops at Trent simply said: the manner of one is bloody and the manner of the other is unbloody. The bishops offered no further explanation. Since the time of Trent, Roman Catholic theologians have developed several competing views on this matter. No one of these competing views has ever been declared official teaching of the church.

Now that we have considered these five preliminary issues on the eucharist, let us turn to the "hierarchy of Catholic truths" which we find in eucharistic theology. First of all, we ask: What is the official teaching of the church on the eucharist? What are those immutable areas of eucharistic doctrine? When religious education teachers draw up their units for the sacrament of the eucharist, they want to be sure that they include all of the official and solemn teachings of the church. The following list is meant to be of help as a teacher prepares the class syllabus on the eucharist.

The Sacrament of Holy Eucharist
Defined Teaching

1. HOLY EUCHARIST IS A SACRAMENT

This can be found in the Council of Trent, *Decree on the Sacraments,* can. 1, in which the seven sacraments are named.

COMMENTS

1. In the entire Christian church, there has never been a major dispute on the main point of this issue. Some Protestant Christian communities will not call the eucharist a "sacrament," but rather an "ordinance." They do this, in part, to avoid the seven-sacrament system of the Roman Catholic Church. The Eastern churches do not call the eucharist a sacrament. For them it is a *divine mystery.* Still, whatever the name, the celebration of the lord's supper is held by almost all Christian communities as one of its two main liturgical rites: baptism and eucharist.

2. Relationship to Christian spirituality. In the eucharist, we celebrate the sacramental presence of Jesus to each of us. This presence of Jesus to us is a gift of grace, not the result of our actions. God so loves us, even with our imperfections, that God wants to be with us in a close, intimate, forgiving and loving way. When we consider our own life, we may say: "Lord, I am not worthy." But God says to each of us, even before we speak: "You are worthy. I want to be with you." Belief in the real presence of Jesus is the center and starting point, not only for all eucharistic theology, but also for all eucharistic spirituality.

2. HOLY EUCHARIST IS A SACRAMENT OF THE PRESENCE OF JESUS

This can be found in the Council of Trent, *Decree on the Eucharist,* can. 1, which speaks of the presence of Jesus as real, true and substantial.

COMMENTS

1. *That* Jesus is truly present in the sacrament of the eucharist is the core of this definition of the church. *How* Jesus is present is not defined.

There are several different theological views which attempt to describe the "how" of this presence. All of them are only theological views; none of them are the official teaching of the church.

2. Relationship to Christian spirituality. Each sacrament is a sacrament **of** something and a sacrament **to** or **for** someone. In the eucharist, the sacrament is a sign or symbol **of** God in Jesus wanting to be present **to** me and **to** all who are gathered around the altar. God is present to me in a deep and personal way; but God is also present in a deep and personal way to each of the Christians who are with me at a eucharistic celebration. Just as we want to be present to those we love, so, too, God wants to be present to me and to all of us because God loves us. Moreover, if we love someone, we continually forgive the imperfections of the one we love. So, too, God continually forgives us our imperfections. The aspects of reconciliation and forgiveness are central to eucharistic spirituality, and they urge us to be forgiving and reconciling to others. The real presence of Jesus in the eucharist is a real presence of a forgiving and compassionate God. In eucharistic theology and spirituality, presence without compassion is meaningless; compassion without presence is also meaningless.

3. THE PRESENCE OF JESUS IS TRUE, REAL AND SUBSTANTIAL

This can be found in the Council of Trent, *Decree on the Eucharist,* can. 1, which uses these precise words for the presence of Jesus.

COMMENTS

1. This teaching of the Council of Trent focuses specifically on the three terms: *true, real and substantial.* Generally, the importance of such terms, and therefore the key to what is being defined, is to consider the opposite of each of these terms: in this definition the opposite of "true" is not false, but imaginary. People often say: "Is that really true or are you making it up?" The presence of Jesus in the eucharist is not something imaginary, something we are making up. Jesus' presence is not due to some memento or reminder, or only some symbolic reference.

The presence is also called "real," and the opposite in this case is "spiritual." "Spiritual" was a term applied to the eucharistic presence and had been so used during the Middle Ages and during the time of the Reformation. The bishops at Trent did not consider a "spiritual presence" adequate to explain the real presence of Jesus in the eucharist. In one sense, the presence of Jesus in the eucharist is very "spiritual," but because this term, spiritual, was used by some authors to downplay the reality of Jesus' eucharistic presence, the bishops emphasized the term, real, over against the term, spiritual. Nonetheless, even today Roman Catholics often speak of a "spiritual communion" in which we pray to Jesus and are spiritually united to Jesus. However, in the eucharist, there is something more than a "spiritual" communion. Jesus is really present to us, not merely in some vague spiritual way but in an actual way.

"Substantial" is a term that comes from the Aristotelian-scholastic philosophical vocabulary, through which eucharistic theology was presented at the time of Trent. Philosophically, the opposite of substance is "accident." But that is not what the bishops intended. We might be present to our loved ones and they to us through a picture or some special reminder. This can happen even when we are "substantially" miles apart. The bishops at Trent did not want to say that Jesus is present to us through some "reminder," but that Jesus *himself* is "substantially" present in the eucharist. It is evident that the three terms, true, real and substantial, all focus on one and the same truth: Jesus himself is personally present in the eucharist.

2. This focus on the "true, real and substantial presence" of Jesus in the eucharist eventually gave rise in Roman Catholicism to an almost exclusive use of the term, "real presence," for the eucharistic presence of Jesus. Today, however, we speak about other "real presences" of Jesus. As yet, theologians have not developed any clear presentation of how all these various "real presences of Jesus" can be integrated.

3. Relationship to Christian spirituality. "True, real and substantial" are very abstract terms when applied to "presence." In day-to-day life, we do not speak about people whom we love being "truly, really and substantially" present to us. More often than not, we speak about presence in terms of "intimacy." In the eucharist, Jesus wants to be intimately close to each of us. Jesus is not simply present by being in the same building as we are or by being physically close to us but not caring about us. Rather, Jesus, in the eucharist, wants to be and is deeply present to us in love and in compassion. Only when we begin to understand the eucharist as a time when Jesus is not distant, but close; not aloof, but very intimate; not above us, but profoundly near us; not judging us, but compassionate toward us, will we truly be able to relate this teaching of the church to our faith and devotion.

4. THE BREAD AND WINE IN THE EUCHARIST ARE NOT MERELY BREAD AND WINE, BUT THEY HAVE BEEN CHANGED INTO THE BODY AND BLOOD OF CHRIST

This is found in the Council of Trent, *Decree on the Eucharist,* can. 2, which speaks of this conversion of the substance of bread and wine into the body and blood of Jesus.

COMMENTS

1. It is crucial to remember in eucharistic catechesis that the teaching of the church on this issue is simply as follows: that the bread and wine are changed into the body and blood of Jesus is the core of the doctrine; how the bread and wine are changed into the body and blood of Jesus is not defined. Theologians have presented many competing views on the "how" of eucharistic change. None of these competing views is the official teaching of the church, but all are acceptable ways of explaining "how" the bread and wine are "changed" into the body and blood of Jesus. Among these theological explanations of how the bread and wine are changed is a traditional view called "transubstantiation," and a contemporary view called "transignification." Each of these two approaches has numerous sub-distinctions and sub-clarifications. In other words, there are several understandings of transubstantiation and there are several understandings of transignification. It is impossible to give a univocal definition of either of these two terms which can then be applied to their many respective subdivisions.

2. The real presence of Jesus is the center of this church teaching. Even a name for this change, *transubstantiation,* though used by the bishops at Trent, was not defined. Consequently, teachers should never say: the teaching of the Roman Catholic Church on the real presence is transubstantiation. Rather, the defined teaching of the church is centered exclusively on the real presence of Jesus in the eucharist.

3. **Relationship to Christian spirituality.** The celebration of every eucharist is a challenge to believe. We have no rational, logical explanation on how Jesus is present. Rather, in faith we say: "Jesus is really present to me. Jesus is really present to us." A Christian, therefore, does not simply "attend" a eucharist but participates in the mystery of the eucharist, and this participation requires faith. When we as Christians say at the eucharist: "Lord, I do believe," then and then only will the eucharist become a

spiritual moment in our lives. Teachers would do well at this juncture of their presentation on the eucharist to spend some time on the meaning of Christian faith today, on the challenges which faith involves, and on the shadow areas of faith. The New Testament phrase: "Lord, I do believe, make firm my unbelief," puts belief and unbelief together. Since so many religious education students go through a challenging time of belief and unbelief, teachers, by spending time on the relationship of eucharist and faith, can truly assist the spiritual journey of their students.

5. THE MASS IS A TRUE SACRIFICE

This can be found in the Council of Trent, *Doctrine on the Holy Sacrifice of the Mass,* can. 1, which states that there is a true and proper sacrifice in the eucharistic celebration.

COMMENTS

1. We have already seen that the bishops at Trent defined that the sacrifice of Jesus was complete and adequate of itself. In their decree on justification, the bishops reiterated the gospel teaching that God alone is the final cause of justification; that God alone is the efficient cause of justification; that Jesus alone is the meritorious cause of justification. In this same decree, it is clearly stated that human nature and human law are impotent to justify anyone; that the very beginning of justification must be based on the prevenient grace of God through Jesus Christ by which people are called through no existing merits of their own, and that none of those things which precede justification, be it faith or good works, can be called the grace of justification. It is primarily through the teaching on the absolute gratutity of God's grace that one is able to state: Roman Catholic doctrine teaches the total and full efficacy of Jesus' sacrifice.

This same position can be based on the rejection by the bishops at Trent of a twofold justification: one being that of Jesus, and the other being that of the Christians themselves. It must be candidly admitted, however, that even with the lengthy debates on twofold justification, the bishops at Trent did not address the full adequacy of Jesus' salvific work in a totally satisfactory way. By rejecting the position that either faith or good works might efficaciously bring about our salvation, and by rejecting a dual-form of justification, the bishops at Trent clearly indicated that the "sacrifice of Jesus," i.e., the efficacy of Jesus' life, death and resurrection for human salvation, is totally God's work. God alone forgives sin. God alone is the efficient and final cause of human salvation.

2. Roman Catholic theologians, however, still struggle to speak in a unified way about the very meaning of the sacrifice of Jesus. *There are no defined teachings on soteriology,* other than the statements in the various creeds which indicate that *for our salvation* the Son of God descended to earth, took on our flesh, suffered death and rose on the third day.

3. In the celebration of the eucharist, the sacrifice of Jesus is not repeated. This sacrifice happened historically once and for all. Some theologians will say that this sacrifice is "re-presented," but when these theologians begin to describe what "representation" means, they express a theological view, not a defined teaching of the church. On the cross and in the eucharist, one can say: the sacrifice is the same; the priest is the same; the offering is the same; the victim is the same. All of these well-known Catholic expressions are trying to say that there is no "second" sacrifice. The one and once-only sacrifice of Jesus is completely efficacious. Never is there a need for a "repetition" of this one sacrifice. Representation can never mean repetition.

Other theologians, today, prefer to say that the eucharist is a sacrament of the one unique sacrifice of Jesus. Still others speak of the *anamnesis* or memorial of the sacrifice of Jesus, in the sense that it is not only a calling to mind of what Jesus did, but an effective proclamation of God's mighty act in Jesus. In other words, one might say that because the eucharist is the memorial of Christ's passover, it is also a sacrifice. Other theologians might word it differently: The eucharist is a sacrifice because it re-presents or makes present the sacrifice of the cross. Still other theologians stress the significance of the eucharist as intercession: the intercession of Jesus, now seated at the right hand of the Father, is at the core of Jesus' sacrifice. In many ways, this view can be found in the letter to the Hebrews. Often, theologians then go on, but in a secondary way, to speak of the intercession of the church. The intercession of Jesus is made on behalf of all men and women, and not simply Christians. The New Testament says: Jesus "died for all." The intercession of the church at the eucharist is united to the great intercession which Jesus in his unique sacrifice once made. However, it can never be said that the church, by this intercession, is the "cause" of salvation. God alone is the cause of our salvation. As every religious education teacher can see, the issue of the eucharist as sacrifice involves many issues of our faith which are difficult to put together into an organic synthesis. There have been and are many theological positions which compete with each other on this matter. Such statements as: the unique sacrifice of Jesus; a sacrifice offered once and for all on the cross—Jesus's sacrifice on Calvary and the eucharist are *one sacrifice*—these are key statements which religious education teachers would do well to emphasize.

4. There are also statements in the works of many Roman Catholic authors, which speak about the sacrifice of the church. These kinds of statements are very ambiguous; they are not necessarily false, but they require considerable nuancing to be understood clearly. Otherwise, statements which emphasize the "unique sacrifice of Jesus," "the once and for all sacrifice of the cross," etc., are called into question. Religious education teachers are well-advised to tread carefully and circumspectly when moving in this direction of a "church's sacrifice." Not even the best of Roman Catholic theologians have been totally clear when they speak about the sacrifice of the church.

5. The exact meaning of the term, sacrifice, is not theologically clear. Some theologians maintain that a sacrifice involves only an offering, while others maintain that both an offering and an immolation belong to the definition of sacrifice. The lack of clarity on the meaning of sacrifice only makes the entire discourse more problematic. If we cannot define "sacrifice," how can we explain the meaning of the "sacrifice" of the mass?

6. Relationship to Christian spirituality. In the past, Christian spirituality which was nourished by the belief that the mass is a sacrifice depended on the more fundamental understanding of the death of Jesus. It was Christology, or more precisely, soteriology, which provided the relationship of eucharist to Christian spirituality. In many catechisms and books, the death of Jesus was presented as the vicarious suffering by Jesus for our sinfulness. The death of Jesus was a vicarious atonement for our sins. The mass was a "re-presentation" of this vicarious offering and immolation. This understanding of the eucharist continues today and many Christians are deeply nourished by it. Without any doubt, one must relate the eucharist to the paschal mystery of Jesus, if one is looking for a relationship to Christian spirituality. The way in which one understands the mystery of Jesus' saving life, death and resurrection will be reflected in the way eucharistic "sacrifice" relates to Christian spirituality. Religious education teachers will have to move beyond a mere sacramental view, and enter into Christology. If a teacher can provide the students with some meaningful ideas on the life, death and resurrection of Jesus, then and then only will the phrase, the eucharist is a sacrifice, begin to nourish their spiritual life. Religious education teachers surely realize that the "vicarious atonement" theory is only one way to understand the death of Jesus. The theory of vicarious atonement has never been defined and there are other equally acceptable ways of understanding the life, death and resurrection of Jesus.

6. IN THE EUCHARISTIC SACRIFICE, JESUS IS BOTH PRIEST AND VICTIM

This can be found in the Council of Trent, *Doctrine on the Holy Sacrifice of the Mass,* chap. 2, in which the bishops state that Jesus is the priest and victim in each eucharistic sacrifice.

COMMENTS

1. This teaching of the church follows from the more general and basic teaching that the eucharistic sacrifice is the same as the unique sacrifice of Jesus. In both, Jesus, and Jesus alone, is the true priest and the victim.

2. If Jesus is the true priest, then the ordained priest, who presides at the liturgy, can only be a sacrament of the one priest, Jesus. Indeed, all that we see, hear, touch and sense in the eucharistic liturgy are sacramental signs of what Jesus' presence is all about. Religious education teachers will find this notion of sacramentality—a sign or symbol **of** something and **to** or **for** someone—very helpful, since the clearer they can indicate the **of what** the eucharist is a sacrament and **for whom** it is a sacrament, the clearer the very reality of eucharist will become. The ordained priest is only a sacrament of the one, true priest. The meal is only a sacrament of the real presence of Jesus. All that one sees is but a sacrament of the reality of Jesus' love and presence. With this understanding of "sacrament," all the sensible data are relativized, and teachers should avoid giving sensible data any absolute value. Only insofar as the perceptible persons and things sacramentalize what the paschal mystery of Jesus is all about, are they effectively sacramental. There is nothing magical or automatic in sacraments. Even when the liturgy is celebrated in a very poor way, the eucharist points to, symbolizes, sacramentalizes the compassionate presence of God in Jesus. It does this not because of any magical words or magical actions or magical people, but because of one thing alone: God has promised to be present to us in Jesus whenever a Christian community assembles and celebrates, even in a poor way, the mystery of eucharist.

3. Relationship to Christian spirituality. The most profound aspect of spirituality which this teaching brings before our minds is this: Whenever we celebrate a sacrament, particularly the eucharist, which we celebrate more frequently than any other sacrament, Jesus is really present. In the eucharist, Jesus, the one and only priest, is present and he is present as priest for us. As priest, he is compassionate and loving; he is just and fair; he is assuring and urging. In the eucharist, Jesus is also the victim, that is, the one whom God accepts on our behalf. In this light, Jesus is the pledge of our future glory and the assurance of our forgiveness. When we speak of Jesus as priest and victim, we are really speaking about the things that God has first done for us, and our only response can be a response, made in faith, of gratitude and love.

The Sacrament of Holy Eucharist
Teachings of the Ordinary Magisterium

There are many teachings and instructions by the ordinary magisterium on the eucharist. The most significant ones are found in the ritual for the celebration of the eucharist and in the revised code of canon law. In these books, regulations for the proper celebration of the eucharist are presented and must be honored as legitimate regulations.

Besides these regulations, there are other official statements of church leadership. Perhaps the ones that are most significant for the eucharist are those which set up the regulations for non-Roman Catholics to receive eucharist with Roman Catholics. Non-uniate Eastern Christians, in cases of need, may receive eucharist in the Roman Catholic Church. In these situations, the priest himself makes the decision, and there is no need for any prior permission from the bishop. Anglicans and Protestants may also receive eucharist at a Roman Catholic eucharistic liturgy. The restrictions are somewhat more exacting, and the bishop's approval is generally required. From a teaching standpoint, the most important issue in all of this is:

In principle, Christians whose baptism we Roman Catholics accept can receive eucharist with us.

In practice, there are various restrictions, but *in principle* intercommunion has been approved. The practical restrictions are merely church regulations and will no doubt vary as time goes on.

Another important aspect of church teaching on the eucharist centers on the placing of the tabernacle. Ideally, there should be a small chapel in which the consecrated eucharist is reserved. In practice, the construction of such a chapel is often not possible. As a result, the tabernacle can be found today in many areas of a church building. However, the tabernacle should never be: (a) on the altar; or (b) in the center directly behind the altar. The reason why the regulations on the placement of a tabernacle is important for eucharistic theology is this: Should we reserve the eucharist? Why should we do so? What is the meaning of praying in front of a tabernacle? The closer one relates eucharistic devotion outside of the eucharist to the actual celebration of the eucharist, the more theologically correct will that devotion be; the more tenuous the relationship is between the reserved sacrament and the actual celebration of the eucharist the more theologically unsound will that devotion be.

The Sacrament of Holy Eucharist
Unresolved Issues

There are many unresolved issues regarding the eucharist, and many of these unresolved issues relate to the sacrament of holy order as well. Many of these unresolved issues relate to the meaning of the priesthood of all believers. Once again, neither theologically nor pedagogically can one give the impression that in the eucharist there are no problems, but only a wonderfully synthesized organic unity. Some of the major unresolved areas are the following:

1. THE RELATION OF BAPTISM TO EUCHARIST

Eucharistic catechesis must be baptismal, just as baptismal catechesis must be eucharistic. The relationship of these two sacraments needs to be further developed. Moreover, the doctrine of faith that we express in our creed—we believe in one baptism—raises ecumenical questions about eucharist. If, in the Roman Catholic Church today, Orthodox Catholics, Anglicans and Protestants can, at times, receive the eucharist, why can they not receive more often?

2. EUCHARIST AND ORDINATION

The validity of ordination in the Anglican and Protestant churches remains a major ecumenical issue which affects the understanding of eucharist among the Christian churches. This issue is still being discussed by theologians. Actually, the issue is far more an ordination issue than a eucharistic issue, since the major point of Roman Catholic discussion on this matter focuses on the validity of ordination in Protestant and Anglican churches. Only when the Roman Catholic leadership will accept the validity of ordination in Anglican and Protestant churches, will the Roman Catholic leadership accept the eucharist in these same churches. Nonetheless, Roman Catholic leadership has stated in several documents, including the documents of Vatican II, that the eucharist in these churches is a very spiritual moment of church life.

3. THE EUCHARIST AND THE PRIESTHOOD OF ALL BELIEVERS

Theologians, since Vatican II, are still reflecting on the role of all baptized Christians in eucharistic celebration. The teaching on the priesthood of all believers and on the ministerial priesthood has not yet been totally clarified. Again, the issue centers more on the sacrament of order than on the sacrament of eucharist, since the relationship between the priesthood of all believers and the ordained priesthood remains a very touchy issue.

4. THE ROLE OF WOMEN IN THE CELEBRATION OF THE EUCHARIST

The role of women in a eucharistic celebration remains an issue of theological discussion. In a number of official church documents, women are allowed to act as a specific minister, but usually when either ordained ministers or baptized males are not available. This reduction of the women's role in eucharistic ministry raises serious questions about the very meaning of Christian discipleship. Are all Christians equal? Are men disciples more equal than women disciples? Does this conform to the New Testament? This issue ranges far beyond the sacrament of the eucharist, although the eucharist appears to be a focus point for all the converging issues. The Vatican "Declaration on the Question of the Admission of Women to the Ministerial Priesthood" [1977] has not ended the discussion on this matter.

5. EUCHARIST AND CULTURE

Inculturation and acculturation of the eucharistic liturgy remains an issue both in practice and in theory. In practice, the Roman Rite is more often than not presented as the norm for all rituals. Ritual equality has not yet been accepted as a practical regulation. Cultural adaptations in eucharistic liturgy are generally judged by their conformity to the Roman Ritual, which is primarily a European construct. The use of various languages in the eucharist does not by itself honestly confront the issues of inculturation and acculturation.

6. THE SEQUENCING OF THE SACRAMENTS

The sequencing of the sacraments remains a problem. Should the sequence be: baptism, penance, eucharist, confirmation? Should it be: baptism, confirmation, eucharist, penance? The *Catechism of the Catholic Church,* with its emphasis on the three sacraments as the sacraments of

Christian initiation, strengthens the view that the flow: baptism, confirmation, eucharist, would be the better approach. Eastern churches have a different sequencing of the sacraments than the Roman Catholic Church has, but the leadership of the Roman Catholic Church has never, in all of church history, declared the other sequencing of the sacraments unacceptable. In theory and in practice, the leadership of the Roman Catholic Church has consistently acknowledged that validity and acceptability of such sequencing as doctrinally and pastorally proper within the Eastern churches.

7. RESERVATION OF THE EUCHARIST

The theology and pastoral practice for reserving the eucharist needs much more refinement. Eucharistic devotions outside of mass have not yet found a clear place in post-Vatican II Roman Catholic life. In practice, parish churches today have little consistency in the ways in which eucharistic devotion outside of the liturgy is celebrated. Dioceses also move in different directions, depending on the preferences of the individual bishops. The conference of bishops has not been able to arrive at a consensus and the few Vatican directives are general and hortative in tone.

Much is asked of religious education teachers as regards their eucharistic catechesis. Since many major eucharistic issues remain theologically unresolved, teachers often find themselves in the crossfire of the debates. Teachers need to know clearly and carefully what must be a part of their eucharistic catechesis (the immutable issues); what is currently required by church leadership; and what issues are still theologically unresolved. Hopefully, the above at least points in that direction and provides religious education teachers with some orientation on these matters.

6

The Sacrament of Holy Reconciliation

There are many aspects to this sacrament of reconciliation, and, con-sequently, there have been many names and words attached to it, such as: conversion, penance, confession, pardon, justification, forgiveness, liber-ation, reconciliation. Each of these names has its own legitimacy, and an over-stress of one without the other diminishes the mystery of God's forgiving love, which this sacrament celebrates. The new ritual for this sacrament does prefer the term, reconciliation, but all the other ideas mentioned above can be found both in the preface and in the prayers of this ritual.

Many students have asked: Why is there a sacrament of reconcilia-tion after baptism? The answer to this question is both easy and difficult. The easy answer is to say that after baptism we are still sinful human beings because of the frailty and weakness of our human nature. This is surely true, but we also know that the eucharist is a sacrament of recon-ciliation and forgives post-baptismal sin and that sin is taken away by an act of perfect contrition. We also know that it was in and through the sacrament of eucharist, not the sacrament of reconciliation, that the vast majority of Christians up to the year A.D. 1000 obtained reconciliation of post-baptismal sin. During their lifetime, the new catechism states, the vast majority of Christians never received even once the sacrament of reconciliation [1447]. If the eucharist during the first half of the church's existence was the normal means for the removal of post-baptismal sin, the question remains: Why is there a specific sacrament of reconciliation for post-baptismal sins? All of this indicates that the answer has a difficult side, as well as an easy side.

A specific sacrament of penance evolved only gradually in church history. Up to the year A.D. 150, we actually have no firm data for the existence of such a sacrament. From the time of the resurrection of Jesus down to the year A.D. 150, theologians have attempted to explain forgiveness of sin within the fledgling church, but all of their positions end up being quite conjectural. After A.D. 150, a public, liturgical ritual of reconciliation gradually developed, but this ritualized action was intended only for the most serious sins. As the catechism itself states: "Christians were rarely admitted [to this sacrament] and in some regions only once in a lifetime" [1447]. Around A.D. 1000 the Celtic form of penance began to be accepted by the church leadership. The Celtic form of penance, made popular by Irish missionaries, was a more private ritual of penance and could be received as often as one wished. The Roman or Mediterranean ritual of penance was a public ritual and could be received only once in a person's lifetime. When the Celtic form of penance had first begun to appear in continental Europe, it had been rejected by the church leadership of Rome. Little by little, the Celtic ritual of reconciliation gradually included the forgiveness of all sins, not just the most serious sins, as was the case in the Roman form. After several stormy centuries of rejection, debate, and discussion, this Celtic form of the sacrament of penance was adopted officially by the Roman church leadership at the Fourth Lateran Council (1215). Only then, and only in the West, did this form of the sacrament become officially mandatory for all serious sins committed after baptism, and for those in serious sin, this sacrament was to be received each year.

The history of this sacrament, with its many variations, counsels one to move cautiously when discussing the sacrament of reconciliation. Once again, religious education teachers will have to consult one of the many well-documented books on the history of the sacrament of reconciliation in order to distinguish more carefully what is "immutable" from what is "changeable."

A religious education teacher will find the four common sacramental issues, stated earlier, to be of great help in making this sacrament meaningful:

1. all sacraments primarily celebrate God's action;

2. all sacraments also primarily celebrate the paschal mystery of Christ;

3. all sacraments are the work of the Holy Spirit;

4. in all sacraments the entire church, *Christus totus,* is the major celebrant of the sacrament.

When the sacrament of reconciliation is presented *primarily as God's action,* not the priest's and not the penitent's; when the sacrament of reconciliation is presented as a *celebration* of the paschal mystery of Christ, and Jesus becomes center-stage of the reconciling process; when the sacrament of reconciliation is presented as a celebration of *the work of the Holy Spirit,* the giver of grace, the one who blesses good deeds; when the sacrament of reconciliation is presented as a ritual in which the main celebrant is the entire church, *Christus totus*—when all of this is presented, then the sacrament of reconciliation begins to be seen in a quite different light.

In order to strengthen this kind of approach to the catechesis on the sacrament of reconciliation, certain key theological issues might be of help to a religious education teacher. These key issues include the following:

1. Only God forgives sin.

   The church in the sacrament of reconciliation celebrates the action of God. As in all sacraments, we celebrate primarily God's action, not our own actions, and therefore the catechesis must stress in a primary way the Christian belief that only God forgives sin.

2. The life, death and resurrection of Jesus is the sacramental basis for this ritualized sacrament.

   The *Introduction* in the new ritual for penance begins with a description of Jesus, "showing forth God's forgiveness of sin." If a teacher does not begin with the Jesus-event as a primary and fundamental reconciling-event, the ritualized sacrament of penance will really make little sense. Jesus, the basic sacrament of a compassionate God, is the primary sacramental foundation for the sacrament of penance.

3. The church, in its prayer, its life, its acts, is a reconciling event.

   In other words, there is something of reconciliation in *everything* that the church does—that is, in everything which Christians, when acting as Christians, do. Reconciliation is not simply one moment in the life of a Christian, nor is it confined to one sacrament of the church. Rather, it is an essential aspect of Christian life on a day-to-day basis. If our students do not experience the Roman Catholic Church as a reconciling reality—and this means, of course, the parish to which they belong—a ritualized celebration of penance will have little meaning. The living church, the parish community with its ecclesiastical leadership, should be a sacrament of a compassionate God. We see once more that even though something very profound and spiritual might be discussed in class, students too often in their daily experience find a parish church leadership or even a diocesan church leadership, which does not reflect the compassion of God. Catechesis on any sacrament is not simply a matter of a religious education class; it must be part of a deeply spiritual renewal at the parish and diocesan level. When these two aspects—the lived-church experience and the ritual of sacramental reconciliation—do not reinforce each other, the enthusiasm of classroom catechesis will be very short-lived.

4. All sin is both an offense against God, and at the same time an offense against others.
   No sin is totally private. There is a social dimension to every sin. Likewise, reconciliation is both a reconciliation with God and a reconciliation with others. When a religious education teacher begins to explain sin in its social dimension, it will be necessary to spend some time on the issue: What is sin? Upper-grade students will certainly raise the social issues of racism and sexism, of violence and injustice. They will question the presence of these social issues not only within the political arena, but also within the church's arena. They will see clearly that the more socially devastating an action is, the more sinful it is, and then they will question the over-emphasis by many church leaders on the sinfulness related to more private sexual matters and the relative silence of these leaders on major social ills, particularly as these social evils affect the internal life of the church. Religious education teachers will have to address these issues of sin, if they hope to make a sacrament of reconciliation meaningful to their students.

5. The passages, Mt. 16:16; 18:18; and Jn. 20:22–23, speak of binding and loosing, but this binding and loosing cannot be restricted only to a ritualized sacramental form of reconciliation.
   There is a power present throughout the church to repel, negate and isolate sin. Forgiveness of sin, binding and loosing, take place whenever and wherever Christian life is in evidence. In Mt. 16:16, a promise is made to Peter. In Mt. 18:18, Jesus is speaking to disciples in general, not simply to the twelve or to the apostles. In Jn. 20:22–23, the text clearly states that Jesus is speaking to the "disciples." Nowhere in the text or context is the group in the upper room limited to the twelve or to the apostles. Nowhere does the Johannine context indicate that only the "twelve" or only

the "apostles" were addressed by Jesus. Today, the best biblical scholarship does not interpret these three passages as a power given exclusively to a leadership group. Nor can these three passages be seen as an institution of the sacrament of reconciliation. Such ideas should never be presented to students for sometime or another in their lives they will read or hear that such a limitation is not what the gospels say. When that happens, their confusion will surely be overwhelming. Nor should these New Testament passages be presented as an occasion when a "special" power was given exclusively to the apostles, which they then passed on to their successors. Although this description of a conferral of special power and its transmission to the apostles' successors has been a "traditional" presentation by many Roman Catholic writers, the best biblical scholarship today makes such a simplistic view totally untenable.

6. The traditional "acts of the pentinent" are three: contrition, confession, and acts of satisfaction.
When a teacher presents the acts of the penitent, care must be taken to follow the official teaching of the church which was stated in the *Decree on Justification* at the Council of Trent.

> Only those theological ways of explaining contrition, confession and satisfaction which maintain the full efficacy of Jesus' salvific action on the one hand, and on the other the full gratuity of God's grace, are conformable to the defined teaching of the Roman Catholic Church.[1]

We are able to make an act of contrition only because God's grace has *first* touched us. We are able to confess our sins because of God's grace. Acts of satisfaction or penances are a response to God's compassionate grace and forgiveness. Reconciliation is indeed a sacrament of forgiveness in which the two parts of this word are deeply important: FOR-giveness, namely God acts first, *before* we even think of making an act of contrition, *before* we even think

---

[1] Kenan Osborne, *Reconciliation and Justification* (New York: Paulist Press, 1990), p. 169.

of confessing our sins, *before* we make any act of penance or satisfaction. For-GIVE, namely, we celebrate in this sacrament primarily what God freely does by way of grace/gift, not what we do by acts of contrition, or confession, or satisfaction.

These are some fundamental or key ideas which may help a teacher construct a syllabus on the sacrament of reconciliation. There are other issues which one must consider as "defined" or "immutable" aspects of the sacrament of reconciliation. The immutable issues dealing with the sacrament of reconciliation are more difficult to formulate than is the case with the other sacramental rituals. In today's liturgy of penance, for instance, there are certain things which are called "essential elements of the sacrament of penance" [cf. *Catechism* 1456]. These "essential elements" must be distinguished at times from the essential or "immutable" elements of our faith. In other words, there are issues which church leadership today *requires* in a ritual of penance, i.e. they are "essential elements." This does not mean automatically that such issues are "immutable verities of one's faith." For instance, private confession to the priest is a church law, not a law of God. In the official and current sacramental structure of penance, private confession to a priest is considered "essential." However, private confession to a priest has not always been required, nor is it required today in the Eastern churches. Although it is "essential" to the Roman Rite of penance today, private confession to a priest is not part of the church's immutable, defined doctrine. Another example would involve the form of priestly absolution. A priest must use the prescribed formula in order that the sacrament be considered valid. The formula of absolution first appeared around the year A.D. 1000, which means that for one thousand years this formula of absolution had not been part of the penitential ritual. Nor is this kind of absolution-formula used in Eastern churches even today, and yet the celebration of reconciliation in these churches is considered "valid" by Roman Catholic leadership. The recitation of the precise formula of absolution used in the Roman Rite is a church law, not a law of God.

Secondly, specifying the exact "defined" doctrines for the sacrament of reconciliation is a difficult task since the specific canons on penance from the Council of Trent require a great deal of background explanation, more so, perhaps, than most other canons of this council. They are not so immediately self-evident and crystal-clear that they could be regarded without further nuancing as "defined doctrine" of the church. At times, theologians themselves do not totally agree on the precise interpretation of these canons on penance. Simply to cite a passage from Trent's *Doctrine on the Sacrament of Penance* does not, by that very fact, indicate a "defined doctrine."

In spite of such limitations and caveats, the following list may be of some assistance to religious education teachers as they formulate their catechesis on the sacrament of reconciliation.

The Sacrament of Holy Reconciliation
Defined Teaching

1. RECONCILIATION IS A SACRAMENT, INSTITUTED BY CHRIST

This can be found in the Council of Trent, *Decree on the Sacraments in General,* can. 1, which lists all seven sacraments. Also in the *Doctrine on the Sacrament of Penance,* can. 1, which states that this is a true and proper sacrament.

COMMENTS

1. In the Roman Catholic Church there is a sacrament of reconciliation. This sacrament does not have the same sacramental rank as baptism and eucharist, but the way in which one sacrament is superior to another has never been defined nor have theologians found an agreeable way to explain the positioning of the sacraments. The sacrament of reconciliation is not the same as the sacrament of baptism, nor is it a "re-profession" of one's baptism. Nonetheless, there remains an integral relationship between the sacraments of baptism and reconciliation, a relationship which has neither been defined (can. 2, *Doctrine on the Sacrament of Penance*), nor unanimously explained by theologians.

2. Moreover, in Roman Catholic theology, this sacrament of reconciliation, as with all the other sacraments, has been "instituted by Christ," which means that it was instituted by God. There is no definition of the Roman Catholic Church on the precise historical moment in the life of Jesus, when Jesus, in his humanity, instituted this sacrament. The passages in the gospels, Mt. 16:16, 18:18 and Jn. 20:22–23, cannot be interpreted as such an historical moment of institution, and religious education teachers should not present these gospel passages as the historical moment when Jesus instituted the sacrament of reconciliation.

3. Relationship to Christian spirituality. When one meditates on the meaning of this church definition: namely, that God is the primary and only cause for this sacramental action and that in this sacramental action one encounters an infinitely compassionate God who forgives sins, one begins to see the depth of God's love for us. God knows of our journey from baptism to death, and God knows that in this journey we often fail. Still, God is a forgiving God. The sacrament of reconciliation is a celebration by the entire church community of God's unfailing love and mercy. The stark words: reconciliation is a sacrament, instituted by God, are words which speak volumes about the very nature of God and God's closeness to us as we struggle through life. In the gospels, Peter asks Jesus: how often must I forgive my brother and sister? Seven times? Jesus answered Peter: Not seven times, but seventy times seven. If we are supposed to forgive our brothers and sisters seventy times seven, then God who is infinite forgives us seventy times seventy times seventy times seventy times seventy. . . . How profound is the mercy and compassion of God!

2. IN THE CHURCH THERE IS A POWER TO FORGIVE SINS

This is found in the Council of Trent, *Doctrine on the Sacrament of Penance,* can. 3, which cites Jn. 20:22–23.

COMMENTS

1. In the teaching of this canon, the power of God to forgive sins cannot be seen primarily or exclusively in an authoritative preaching of the gospel, a view which some of Luther's followers held. This power must also be acknowledged as operative in the sacrament of penance, though not in an exclusive way. In other words, the power over sin, which is evident throughout the Christian church, is also evident in the sacrament of reconciliation. Some of the Protestants at the time of Trent were denying any effective forgiveness in the sacrament of reconciliation as it was celebrated in the Roman church. The focus of this canon was to offset such a denial.

2. Relationship to Christian spirituality. One of the most remarkable aspects we find in the lives of the saints is their personal expression of being sinful. Men and women whom we regard as very holy people have called themselves "the greatest of sinners." Ordinary Christians like ourselves cannot help but wonder: If these most holy men and women are the "greatest sinners," then what kind of sinners are we, the ordinary, less holy people? Slowly we begin to see that we are people who simply do not realize what sin truly is. We are so accustomed to the evil in our life that we do not even think of it any longer as evil or sinful. Saints, who are attuned in a sensitive way to the ever-present love and mercy of God, are much more sensitive to the presence of sin, to those aspects of one's life which destroy a relationship to this loving and caring God. In the Christian church, we are asked by this official teaching to become more sensitive to the presence of a forgiving God throughout the entire fabric of church life, and then to celebrate God's forgiveness in a special way with love and humility whenever we celebrate the sacrament of reconciliation. This sacrament should never be drudgery. It should never be a moment of fear and pain. It should be a celebration. In the past, the ritual has encouraged too much drudgery, fear, and pain; in the new rituals the encouragement is toward the celebration by the entire church, *Christus totus.*

3. AN ACT OF PERFECT CONTRITION IS THE OCCASION WHEN ALL SERIOUS SIN IS FORGIVEN

This is found in the Council of Trent, *Doctrine on the Sacrament of Penance,* can. 5, which states that an act of perfect contrition takes away all serious sin and any eternal punishment which serious sin incurs.

COMMENTS

1. From the time of Peter Abelard, a theologian in the twelfth century, there has been an ongoing discussion on the role of a perfect act of contrition in the process of reconciliation. All theologians and canonists agreed that an act of contrition took away serious sin and its eternal punishment, and this was restated officially by the Council of Trent. Whenever a person repents of sin, not merely to avoid the punishment of hell, but because sin has offended God, God forgives that person's sin. This is the focus of this defined truth.

2. What is not defined and what remains a matter of theological speculation is the way in which such an act of contrition is part of the process of reconciliation. How does an act of contrition relate to the sacrament of penance? If one's serious sins are taken away by an act of perfect contrition, why is it necessary to "go to confession"? It is this relationship which has never been defined and which remains today theologically disputed. Religious education teachers will not have a satisfactory resolution to this issue. Minimally, one can say that the further confession of one's sin in the sacrament of penance is a regulation or law of the church. However, there may be deeper theological reasons for this, and several ways have been proposed by theologians. Franciscan and Dominican theologians have proposed the two most important competing views. Franciscans have emphasized a forgiveness of sin with no relationship at all to the sacrament of reconciliation. Dominican theologians have emphasized a relationship of sin, in all cases, to the sacrament of reconciliation. Neither of these theological positions, nor any other theological position on this issue, however, should be presented to a class as the defined teaching of the church.

   3. Relationship to Christian spirituality. We believe that only God forgives sin, and that God turns us away from sin through grace. When this happens, we speak of a conversion, a conversion away from sin and to God. The teaching of the church on perfect contrition turns our attention to this working of God's free grace in the depths of our conscience. The Second Vatican Council writes in *Gaudium et Spes:*

> Deep within one's conscience, a person discovers a law which one has not laid on oneself, but which one must obey. Its voice, ever calling one to love and do what is good and to avoid evil, tells one inwardly at the right moment: do this, shun that. . . . Conscience is a person's most secret core and sanctuary. There one is alone with God, whose voice echoes in one's depth [16].

God is present at our most innermost depths, urging us to goodness and holiness. God's action of forgiving sins takes place in this most sacred core and sanctuary of our being. This is what contrition is all about: the presence of a forgiving God acting at the deepest dimensions of our human life.

4. CONFESSION OF ONE'S SINS IS A NECESSARY PART OF RECONCILIATION

   This is found in the Council of Trent, *Doctrine on the Sacrament of Penance,* can. 4, which mentions the three acts of the penitent: contrition, confession and satisfaction, and can. 7, which addresses the confession of sins in a more specific way.

COMMENTS

   1. There is a certain amount of misunderstanding about this issue of confession of one's sins: namely, what precisely is "defined" and "immutable," and what is only a prescription of "church law" and is therefore "changeable." Too often it has been taught: (a) that one must confess all sins privately to a priest in species and number, and (b) that this is the "defined teaching of the Roman Catholic Church." This is not the case at all and religious education teachers must carefully make some important distinctions.

2. "Confession of one's sins" is indeed a necessary part of the process of reconciliation. Confession means, in the first place, that a sinner acknowledges that he or she is a sinner. Even more one must acknowledge all one's serious sins. Confession of one's serious sins can never be a confession of only a specific serious sin and a non-confession of certain other serious sins. The confession of one's sinfulness must be "integral," i.e., it must be a confession of all one's serious sins. If we are not sorry for all our serious sins and if we expect God to forgive us only those serious sins which we want to confess, then we are asking God to be a "capricious God," a God who picks and chooses what is evil and what is not evil on the basis of what we choose as evil and not evil. The phrase: confession of one's sins, means first of all an "integral" confession of all our serious sins.

3. There is no defined doctrine of the faith in the Roman Catholic Church that by divine law all serious sins must be confessed privately to a priest in species and number. Such a private confession to a priest is not part of divine law; it is part of church law only. This distinction does not mean that such private confession is unimportant, but it does mean that it is not required by divine law, and, as a result, such private confession is not absolutely "essential" to the sacrament of reconciliation. In today's church law there is a regulation of the Roman Catholic Church that this is the presently prescribed mode for confessing one's serious and substantive sins. Such a regulation is not the case in most Eastern churches, and there is no such regulation in Anglican and Protestant churches. Religious education teachers should make the meaning of this phrase: *confession of one's sins*, quite clear to students, and also make it quite clear that the private mode of confessing one's sins is of church law, not divine law.

4. Relationship to Christian spirituality. Whenever we confess our sinfulness and are sorry for all our serious sins, we are first of all acknowledging the holiness of God. God is holy and does not traffic in sin. Our unholiness is a trafficking in sin. Confession of one's sins is really an acknowledgement in faith of an all-holy God. Second, confession of our sinfulness which includes all of our serious sins against God is an acknowledgement of God's great compassion. Why would we ever make such a confession if we did not believe that God would, in love and mercy, be a forgiving God of all our serious sins? In our attempt to relate this teaching of the church to Christian spirituality, the focus should be God-centered, not human-centered. It should not be on a "searching our conscience" for all possible sinfulness; rather, it should be searching into the very depths of God's own mercy and love, a depth and breadth which reaches out to every area of our own sinful life and fills that life, unworthy though it is, with forgiving grace.

5. ACTS OF SATISFACTION ARE PART OF THE PROCESS OF RECONCILIATION

This is found in the Council of Trent, *Doctrine on the Sacrament of Penance,* can. 14, which speaks of our human acts of satisfaction as honoring God.

COMMENTS

1. Great care must be taken by all teachers to relate any catechesis on "satisfaction" with the *Decree on Justification,* which the Council of Trent promulgated. In that decree, it is crystal-clear that there is an absolute gratuity to God's grace. In other words, one must be very careful when using any terms like "satisfaction" or "merit," or "earning grace." If God's grace is absolutely gratuitous, that is free, then we really do not "merit," "satisfy," or "earn" grace, in any strict sense of these terms.

2. Positively stated, this official and defined teaching of the church tells us that our human behavior should really bear witness to the presence of God's free gift of grace in our lives. This response to God's forgiving action has been traditionally called "satisfaction." When presented as a response in gratitude to God's free act of forgiving grace, there is no problem. Indeed, there is only worship and honor given to God. When, on the other hand, this response is presented as partly "causing," partly "satisfying," partly "meriting" God's forgiveness of our sins, then there is a major problem, since in such a presentation grace ceases to be grace. Gift ceases to be gift.

3. Relationship to Christian spirituality. Prayer begins with wonder and amazement at the overwhelming love of God. Spirituality is fundamentally a response to God's loving and forgiving presence. When we realize, even in our day-to-day life, that a person loves us and loves us deeply, we respond to that love by expressions of gratitude. We know that we cannot purchase or merit or earn someone's love. Love is always a gift. God's forgiveness is an even greater gift of love to us, and our only response can be one of wonder, amazement, and gratitude. If a person experiences the love of God and then turns around and offends God again and again through continued sin, has one really understood God's love? If in our day-to-day love we say that we are glad that someone loves us, but then turn around and offend that person again and again, have we really understood how much the other person loves us? Is not our acknowledgement of the other person's love mere lip-service? We cannot honor God by mere lip-service. We honor God by a life of holiness, which is a reflection in our life of the very holiness of God. This, and this alone, is what "satisfaction" truly is.

6. ALL POST-BAPTISMAL SINS CAN BE FORGIVEN

This can be found in the Council of Trent, *Doctrine on the Sacrament of Penance,* can. 1, which says that all post-baptismal sins can be forgiven.

COMMENTS

1. The focus of this teaching is once again much more on our belief in God than on the sacrament of reconciliation. Evil is never greater than God. There is no sin which goes beyond God's infinite compassion. The meaning of the scriptural passage which speaks of a sin "against the Holy Spirit" remains very unclear and no implications can be drawn from the passage. Every interpretation, even if made by the best biblical scholars, is highly tentative.

2. Relationship to Christian spirituality. What hope this offers to all of us in our spiritual journey! The mercy of God is never outpaced by the misery of human life. Augustine once used a play on words: mercy, in Latin, *misericordia,* and misery, in Latin, *miseria.* In our misery/*miseria,* he writes, we seem to be running away from God, but as we run away, we find that God in mercy/*misericordia* is running not after us, but ahead of us and running to meet us. We can never run away from the mercy of God. God's goodness is infinite and unlimited; evil is always limited and limiting. The mystery of grace is unlimited and unlimiting. Evil is never the final answer; God's grace and mercy always remain the final answer.

7. THE ORDAINED PRIEST THROUGH ABSOLUTION IS PART OF THE PROCESS OF RECONCILIATION

This is found in the Council of Trent, *Doctrine on the Sacrament of Penance,* can. 9, in which the bishops stress that the role of priestly absolution is part of the process of reconciliation.

COMMENTS

1. Some of the Protestant theologians at the time of the Reformation taught that priestly absolution had little or no meaning for the forgiveness of sin. The bishops at Trent stated that this was not correct church teaching and that priestly absolution was a central part of the reconciliation process. Roman Catholic theologians at that same time were not in agreement as to the precise way in which priestly absolution was integrated into the reconciliation process. As a result, one must say: that priestly absolution as part of the process of reconciliation is a defined doctrine of the church; how priestly absolution fits into the reconciliation process has never been defined.

2. In the new ritual for reconciliation, the prayer of priestly absolution was reconstructed in a very careful way. This prayer begins with salvation history from the beginning of creation, down to the paschal mystery in the life, death and resurrection of Jesus, to the presence of the Spirit of God in the church itself. Only against this background of salvation history are the words added: "and therefore, I forgive you in the name of the Father, and of the Son and of the Holy Spirit." In other words, these priestly words of absolution have their meaning only within the context of salvation history, and the newly constructed prayer of priestly absolution brings this out in a very deliberate way. By placing the prayer of absolution within this context, the emphasis is more on God's activity than on any magical words which a priest might say. Indeed, the words of the priest are meaningless unless they are sacraments or symbols of God's salvific action.

3. Relationship to Christian spirituality. Perhaps at this juncture it might be opportune to say that the entire spirituality for this sacrament of reconciliation rests on Christology. Unless one has begun to appreciate the compassionate Jesus, the spirituality in this sacrament will never be realized. A religious education teacher must be "turned on" by Jesus. Every page of the New Testament speaks about reconciliation. Jesus preached reconciliation. Jesus lived reconciliation. His death was a moment of reconciliation. The resurrection is a reconciling-event. Christian spirituality is centered in Jesus. As a result, a religious education teacher would benefit the catechesis for this sacrament by spending a lengthy period of time on Jesus in whose message and in whose life, death and resurrection, one experiences God's forgiving grace.

Second, a religious education teacher must spend a lengthy period of time on the mystery of the church as a mystery of reconciling love. Somehow, one must anchor one's faith in the church at a very profound level, a level far beneath the pettiness of some church life and far beneath the unforgiving approach of some church people. My faith cannot depend on how others, even ecclesiastical others, lead their lives. My faith in the church must be anchored in a depth of this mystery called church in which one finds a reflection of Jesus and of God's forgiving love. The contemporary presentation of the church as basic sacrament helps in this matter, since whenever the church reflects Jesus it is truly church. The very title of the document from Vatican II, *Lumen Gentium,* means that Jesus is the light of the world. When the church reflects Jesus, the church is truly the mystery of this light, the sacrament of Jesus himself, who, in his humanity, is the very sacrament of a compassionate God.

Only with this Christology of reconciliation and this ecclesiology of reconciliation will the sacrament of reconciliation be spiritually and theologically of value. That is why a catechesis on the sacrament of reconciliation which hopes to be spiritually enriching must include in a very strong way a spiritual understanding of the reconciling Jesus and the reconciling church.

The Sacrament of Holy Reconciliation
Teachings of the Ordinary Magisterium

There are several main documents which present the teachings of the ordinary magisterium on the sacrament of reconciliation. The primary document is, of course, the revised ritual for this sacrament, with its three liturgical forms and a fourth form to be used in the emergency of death. There are also other documents: (1) *Normae Pastorales: Sacramentum paenitentiae,* issued by the Sacred Congregation of the Faith [1972], a document which provides norms for general absolution; (2) a letter from this same congregation [Jan. 14, 1977] to the bishops of the United States, with additional comments on the pastoral norms for general absolution; (3) a joint declaration from two congregations, the Sacred Congregation for the Discipline of the Sacraments and the Sacred Congregation for the Clergy, *Sanctus Pontifex,* which discusses first reconciliation prior to first eucharist; (4) a clarification on first reconciliation, *In quibusdam Ecclesiae partibus,* which the two congregations sent to the bishops of the United States; and (5) *Omnis utriusque* of Lateran IV, with its regulation for annual confession. All of these documents contain certain aspects of the ordinary magisterium. Finally, the revised code of canon law has a section on the sacrament of reconciliation, with a variety of canons. This, too, is part of the ordinary magisterium.

These documents do not exhaust the material of the ordinary magisterium on the issue of the sacrament of penance. Of major importance are those parts of the Vatican II documents which set up norms for sacramental celebrations. These norms were cited above in the section on sacraments in general, but they apply with vigor to the celebration of this sacrament. A major norm was this: communal celebration of the sacraments is preferred to more private celebrations. This conciliar norm, however, has been juxtaposed with almost an opposing regulation by the ordinary magisterium which time and again stresses "private" confession.

Religious education teachers must continually realize that all the above documents are ordinary magisterium, that is, they are official documents, but they do not *per se* present any immutable teachings of the church. Immutable teachings might be included in these documents, but the documents themselves are official, but changeable. The changeable material in these documents should be presented to religious education students as official, but changeable.

The Sacrament of Holy Reconciliation
Unresolved Issues

There are currently five major unresolved issues which deal with the sacrament of reconciliation. There are other unresolved issues as well, but these seem to be the more imperative issues for today's religious education.

1. GENERAL ABSOLUTION

Even though the official ritual of the Roman Catholic Church has allowed a greater role for general absolution within the framework of church life, there remains a tendency on the part of current church leadership to restrict the use of general absolution. This is done in a number of ways. There is considerable debate over the well-used phrase "case of necessity" and its application to general absolution. This phrase is highly ambiguous, since on the one hand every celebration of this sacrament can be seen as a "case of necessity," and on the other hand, the new ritual has a fourth form for those cases of necessity which involved life-and-death matters. The debates over the length of time which would occur if general absolution were not given and a person would subsequently have the opportunity for private confession have ended up in an arbitrary judgement. The bishops of the United States have selected a thirty-day period, but as one can see this is simply an arbitrarily chosen length of time.

Secondly, when one validly receives general absolution, one has made an "integral confession," since there cannot be a valid celebration of this sacrament which would not involve "integral confession." This means that "integral" is not the same as "private confession of all serious sins to a priest in species and number." There is not an agreement either by theologians or by hierarchical leadership on the meaning of "integral," and as a consequence when this is used in the discussions on general absolution, there is no common base of discourse.

Thirdly, the requirement after a valid general confession to "confess" all already-forgiven serious sins to a priest in private confession, in accordance with the regulations of the new ritual, is very difficult to substantiate. Clearly, one can say it is a "law of the church." Beyond that basis, a clear and sound theological necessity for such an additional confession of previously confessed sins is difficult to develop with any cogency.

All of this leaves religious education teachers in a sort of limbo. Is general absolution acceptable or not? Why are there apparently unnecessary restrictions placed on the celebration of penance in this way? If a communal form of a sacrament is preferable to all other forms, why is this communal form of general absolution not endorsed more readily by church authority? Why are teachers receiving "mixed messages" on this matter?

2. PRIVATE CONFESSION TO A PRIEST

Enough has been said already in the above pages to indicate that there are basic theological problems with private confession to a priest. The most telling of these problems is that private confession of serious sins in species and number to a priest is not of divine law but only of church law. The situation becomes more problematic whenever this church requirement is presented to the Christian community as divine law or as absolutely necessary. Secondly, since perfect contrition by itself takes away all sin, the connection between perfect contrition and the absolution given by a priest has been an issue, which theologians since A.D. 1100 have continued to debate and to date have not arrived at any satisfactory resolution. All theological answers to date are opinions and competing opinions at that. Religious education teachers, consequently, cannot hope to present an "organic synthesis" on this issue to their students, and yet the issue lies at the very heart of sacramental reconciliation.

3. THE AGE FOR FIRST RECONCILIATION

There is only one law of the church on the issue: When is sacramental confession necessary? This was stated by the Lateran IV Council in 1215 and this conciliar statement is often cited today by church authority. The rule is this: a Roman Catholic, aware of serious sin, must confess to a priest if this is physically and morally possible. There is no other time when a Roman Catholic, of any age, must confess to a priest. To require children to go to the sacrament of reconciliation prior to the reception of first eucharist stands in opposition to this single law of the church. A teacher can only say that this is another and new regulation of the church, but a teacher also knows that no Catholics, including children, have to go to confession prior to communion, unless they are fully aware of serious sin and have the physical and moral possibility of confessing to a priest. On the one hand, there is a rule, but on the other hand there is neither rule nor can there be a rule. Such is the dilemma which one faces on this issue of requisite first confession prior to first eucharist. Church leadership has its own problem in this matter: How can church leadership establish a regulation which theologically and canonically is unnecessary?

4. THE ISSUE OF FREQUENT CONFESSION

This is basically a problem which affects the meaning of priesthood. In the theology of priesthood which Vatican II officially endorsed, the primary task of a priest is to proclaim the gospel. Of the three offices— prophet, priest and king (teacher/preacher, sanctifier, leader)—the primary office is that of prophet or teacher/preacher. More time and effort should be given by priests and bishops to this office and task than to any other task. Secondly, if a priest or bishop follows the new ritual properly— the ritual says in Latin "*rite*"—an individual celebration of the sacrament would normally take about four to five minutes. If it is not done according to the ritual but abbreviated, then the renewal of the sacrament of reconciliation itself is thwarted. On the other hand, if priests and bishops take the proper time to "hear confessions," then an injunction for frequent confession places the priest and bishop in an untenable position. He would of necessity have to spend longer hours "hearing confessions," and therefore less hours would be devoted to his primary task of preaching the gospel. Clearly, this is a situation of "mixed signals" coming from the Vatican itself. If teachers encourage their students to practice "frequent confession," then the teachers themselves are compounding the problem. There is to date no resolution of this very mixed-signalled situation.

5. JUSTIFICATION AND THE SACRAMENT OF RECONCILIATION

An enormously complex theological problem is the relationship between the decree on justification, which the Council of Trent promulgated, and the sacrament of reconciliation. The bishops at Trent made no effort to relate these two aspects of Christian life, and since the time of Trent there has been little effort on the part of the hierarchical leadership of the church or the theologians to do so. Only with the ecumenical discussions, particularly between Roman Catholics and Lutherans, has the theme of justification once more entered into a central focus for Roman Catholics. Unless this interrelationship is more carefully put together, the problematic areas indigenous to the sacrament of reconciliation will not be resolved. Religious education teachers cannot be held responsible to bring about this resolution. The hierarchy and the theologians have this responsibility. However, religious education teachers will experience the tensions which exist, since the two issues have not been satisfactorily interrelated.

7

The Sacrament of Holy Anointing

Since the renewal of the sacraments after Vatican II, the sacrament of the anointing of the sick has experienced deep changes. The very name for this sacrament has been changed: from extreme unction, which describes a sacrament for the dying, to anointing of the sick, which describes a sacrament for those who are ill. A mere change of name, however, does not mean an automatic change in the theology behind the sacrament, nor in the everyday experience of Christians as regards this sacrament.

Religious education teachers, however, will still find several areas which present major difficulties in the catechesis for this sacrament. Some of the more important major difficulties regarding the sacrament of anointing include:

1. NO ADEQUATE THEOLOGY OF SICKNESS

Within Roman Catholic theology, there is to date no adequate theology of sickness. There is, however, a well-developed theology of death, formulated by K. Rahner, L. Boros, and C. Troisfontaines. But for sickness, there is no similar theological understanding. Theologians who write on sickness have presented several disparate directions for a Christian understanding of sickness. These presentations fluctuate between a this-worldly approach and an other-worldly approach. Even the new ritual witnesses to this type of theological fluctuation. Illness has been presented as a preparation for heaven, a means of suffering in this present life, so that one might be rewarded in heaven. At other times, illness has been presented as a normal part of human life, but it is a part of human life because of sin. Had there been no sin, so this understanding goes, there would have been no illness. Even the example of Jesus has often been used to give some explanation of illness: Jesus was moved by the suffering of people and was widely regarded as a healer. Jesus was called the physician. Because of this, some theologians and other writers have said, Jesus has given a new meaning to illness. Illness, from this standpoint, can make us more like Jesus and through sickness we are united to his own redemptive suffering. Every catechesis on this sacrament will probably continue to be a difficult task for some time since an adequate theological explanation of the meaning of sickness still remains elusive.

2. HISTORICAL PROBLEMS THAT LINGER ON

The history of this sacrament has been very diverse and several key issues which are stressed today as almost "essential" were not considered "essential" over long stretches of Christian living. In the history of this sacrament, the key period for change took place in the Carolingian period of renewal [A.D. 751–1000]. During this time, major steps were taken which altered the sacramental rite in very substantive ways. There is no extant historical data during the period 751–1000, which pinpoint precise "moments" of such changes. Rather, one must consider the approach to this sacrament as it appears in the eighth century, and then contrast this view of anointing of the sick with the approach to the sacrament as it appears in the eleventh century.

IN THE EIGHTH CENTURY	IN THE ELEVENTH CENTURY
1. All Christians could anoint. Men and women, ordained and non-ordained anointed.	Only priests could anoint. Deacons and all lay people were forbidden to anoint.
2. A Christian suffering almost any illness could be anointed and anointed frequently.	Only Christians near death were anointed. Second anointings for the same illness were not allowed.
3. Healing of the body was the major effect of this sacrament.	Forgiveness of sin was the major effect of this sacrament.
4. Children and infants were anointed as well as adults.	Only those Christians who could commit mortal sin could be anointed.

It is obvious from this diagram that major changes took place during the Carolingian reform. These changes were not mandated or orchestrated by Rome. Rather, the changes gradually found their way into the pastoral ministry of the church, first through local churches and local customs, then through regional structures of church life, and only at the end of the Carolingian period did the changes become fairly uniform throughout the Western Roman Catholic Church. Upon analysis, it is obvious that the one key issue which determined all the others was number three, namely, the issue of forgiveness of sin. Once forgiveness of sin became the primary effect of this sacrament, then all the other changes fell into place: that is, only priests, who had the lawful jurisdiction to forgive sins, could anoint; only those Christians who had reached the age of reason and, therefore, capable of mortal sin could be anointed; only one anointing per each serious illness, since sins are forgiven only once. When anointing of the sick became a sacrament of the forgiveness of sin, the sacrament was clericalized and theologians of that era proceeded to give a theological basis for a clericalized sacrament of the anointing of the sick. Both this history and its theological justification remain operative, to some degree, in the way this sacrament has been renewed. Some of the major issues behind the Vatican II renewal of the sacraments and key issues in its history and its theological justification tend to go in opposite directions. As a result, the catechesis for this sacrament also moves in diverse directions, since it includes some incompatible material.

3. THE RELATIONSHIP BETWEEN THE SACRAMENT OF ANOINTING AND THE SACRAMENT OF RECONCILIATION

Once the historical changes took place, i.e., changes from a sacrament primarily intended for physical healing, administered by all baptized Christians and to all baptized Christians, to a sacrament primarily intended for the forgiveness of sin, restricted to the ministry of a priest and to Christian people capable of serious sin, theologians of the Middle Ages had to distinguish the sacrament of anointing with its peculiar forgiveness of sin from the sacrament of reconciliation with *its* peculiar forgiveness of sin. Eventually, this kind of theologizing led to the distinction between a sacrament which was primarily instituted to forgive serious sin, i.e., reconciliation or penance, and a sacrament which only tangentially was instituted to forgive serious sin, i.e., anointing of someone who was physically or morally unable to make a confession. This latter sacrament was instituted, nonetheless, with some relationship to the forgiveness of serious sin. Medieval theologians found a further distinction helpful in this matter: the sacrament of reconciliation or penance was instituted to forgive actual sin as well as all eternal punishments due to sin; the sacrament of anointing was instituted to forgive the temporal punishments still due to serious sin, once such sin had been forgiven in the sacrament of penance. This line of theological thought eventually gave rise to the name "extreme" anointing or "extreme" unction. In one's day-to-day Christian life, the sacraments of reconciliation and eucharist provided all the necessary sacramental and spiritual help which a Christian might need for the remission of sin. At the time of death, however, something more was needed to insure the happy passage of a soul from this life to the next. The sacrament of "extreme" unction became the sacrament for the dying. A Franciscan theologian, John Duns Scotus, considered the sacrament of anointing as a substitute for purgatory. Every Christian who received this sacrament worthily at the moment of death bypassed purgatory altogether and went straight to heaven. This view was the most "extreme" theological explanation of "extreme unction." Still, it was quite popular and gave rise to several other names for this sacrament: sacrament of glory, sacrament of the resurrection, sacrament of eternal life. In our own century, only twenty to thirty years prior to Vatican II, these various names were advocated anew by many well-known and highly influential Roman Catholic theologians as names that expressed the essential meaning of the sacrament of anointing.

In the renewal of this sacrament after Vatican II, the issue of forgiveness of sin remains operative. Since this sacrament forgives sin, deacons may not anoint, and every recent request to the Vatican to allow deacons to anoint has been refused. Even less acceptable is the possibility of lay men and women anointing. All of these requests have been rejected, even though in the history of the Roman Catholic Church, lay men and lay women were the ministers of anointing the sick for about 800 or 900 years, and the non-ordained were anointing the sick of that time with the full encouragement and approval of church leadership, including the leadership at Rome. Today, we may have non-ordained ministers of the eucharist and non-ordained ministers of the word, but we do not have non-ordained ministers of the sick who can anoint, precisely because in the post-Vatican II renewal forgiveness of sin remained an operative factor within this sacramental ritual. The argument seems to move as follows: anointing of the sick forgives sin. If deacons and lay men and women were allowed to anoint, then they would share in the power to forgive sin, a power exclusively reserved to priests. Church leadership would have then allowed to the baptized-at-large a "power" reserved to the ordained priest. A religious education teacher notices at once that the focal issue is no longer an issue dealing with the sacrament of the anointing of the sick, but an issue about clerical power within the church.

4. THE HISTORY OF THE ORIGIN OF THE SACRAMENT OF THE ANOINTING OF THE SICK

The use of oil for medicinal purposes was widespread throughout the Middle East. In many ways, it was the "aspirin" of the time, that is, the most common medicine in use. However, not all healing involved the use of oil. Thus, in the many healings of Jesus, more often than not, no mention is made of oil or anointing. Nonetheless, Jesus the healer was one of his most treasured titles, and Christian literature in the two centuries after the resurrection frequently makes mention of Jesus the healer.

In Jewish medicine, which was borrowed basically from the Egyptians, there was no role for purely "secular" medicine. Often in the Old Testament we are reminded that *the* physician is God. Medicines and doctors in the early Jewish view were only secondary causes when there is a healing process. It was primarily God who healed, using at times the efforts of physicians and the power of various medicines. Against the background of Yahweh as *the healer,* the miracles of Jesus are seen as events that emphasize the presence of God in Jesus. The story of the man born blind in Jn. 9 is an excellent example of these issues: the power of God, the miracle of Jesus, the issue of sin and the devil, the issue of God's action alone. The Jewish background undergirds each of Jesus' healings. It is God who heals and Jesus is the holy one of God. To acknowledge that Jesus healed was an acknowledgement that God was present in Jesus.

In the letter of James, a document often cited when the sacrament of anointing is discussed, the role of the elders is unclear. Neither the text itself, nor the context, offers any clarity. There is no possible way that these elders (*presbyters*) can be identified with the later emergence of Christian presbyters. When one moves beyond the New Testament, one finds at best a few historical indications during the first five centuries of the Christian church that oil was blessed by a bishop so that people could take it home and anoint those who were ill. Efforts to "find" this sacrament in the sacred history of the Old Testament or in passages on healing in the New Testament tend to be more conjectural than substantial. Religious education teachers should be very circumspect and cautious as they describe the history of this sacrament. Well-crafted books which deal with this history will be especially needed to provide a balanced historical overview of this sacrament.

5. AN INTEGRATION INTO THE SACRAMENT OF ANOINTING TO THE FOUR COMMON SACRAMENTAL ISSUES MENTIONED EARLIER

The four common themes of all liturgical and sacramental worship are often not integrated into various presentations of this sacrament, but these four issues will clearly help a religious education teacher develop a meaningful approach to this sacrament.

1. The action of God is primary.

   Since all sacraments are primarily the celebration of God's action, and not a celebration of our human actions, the sacrament of anointing is no different. In this sacrament, we celebrate the love of God for us, even when we are sick, even when we are seriously sick. This action of God is an action which stresses life, not death. God wants us to be healthy, and God gives us the grace of health. When our human life has run its course, God is still life-affirming, but at this moment of time the affirmation becomes an affirmation of life beyond our present human life. Clearly, a distinction must be made in the ritual between an affirmation of God's action for the ups and downs in the health of a person, and an affirmation of God's action in terminally ill cases. Perhaps, sometime in the future, we will have two different rituals for this holy sacrament.

2. All sacraments primarily celebrate the paschal mystery by which Christ saved us.

   The mystery of Jesus is a mystery of life and the paschal mystery is a mystery of risen life, not only in some dim future after one's death, but in the here-and-now of our this-worldly life. The paschal mystery celebrates the presence of Jesus in our lives whether we are holy or whether we have strayed from the gospel through sin; whether we are full of vigor and health or whether we are marginated by illness and pain. If we truly believe that Jesus preached the kingdom of God as present NOW, and not simply in the HEREAFTER, then this "now" extends to the now of pain, the now of loneliness, the now of mental illness, the now of physical illness, the now of any illness. God in Jesus is with us in all these "nows" of our life, urging us to live as best we can with the help of his compassionate and unending grace.

3. In all sacraments the Holy Spirit makes Christ present to the church.

The Holy Spirit is the very reason why this sacrament should be called "holy anointing." The Spirit of Jesus hallows the oil, hallows the prayers, hallows the gathered community, hallows the various ministers, and above all hallows the one who is sick. This Spirit of Jesus is the Spirit of wisdom and fortitude, the Spirit of life and health. In this sacrament, we are celebrating the presence of the Spirit who brought life out of chaos, who swooped down like a bird over Jesus, who made the blind see and the lame walk. Whenever we celebrate holy anointing, all of us, the person sick and those around, are in the presence of holiness. God is present and active; we can only answer: "Bless God! We turn to you. We trust in you. We love you."

4. All sacraments are an action of the whole Christ, *Christus totus.* In the celebration of this sacrament, the main celebrant is the whole Christ, not those who proclaim the word or administer the oil. The whole Christ is in each and all: the one who is ill and the ones who are gathered. Once again, we are celebrating the real presence of the physician, Jesus, who heals the sick and binds up their infirmities. In the celebration of this sacrament, our response must be that of faith: Lord Jesus, physician and healer, we do believe, make firm our unbelief.

When these four "common" issues are brought into a discussion of the sacrament of the anointing of the sick, such expressions as "primary," *Christus totus,* and "the action of the Holy Spirit" will give a quite different tone and stress as one emphasizes what is "immutable" in the sacrament and what is "changeable."

Sacrament of Holy Anointing
Defined Teaching

1. ANOINTING OF THE SICK IS A SACRAMENT OF THE CHURCH

This is found in the Council of Trent, *Decree on the Sacraments in General*, can. 1, in which all seven sacraments are mentioned. This is also found in the *Doctrine on the Sacraments of Extreme Unction*, can. 1. In both of these documents the bishops state unequivocally that "extreme unction" is a sacrament of the church.

COMMENTS

1. That the anointing of the sick is one of the sacraments of the Christian church is the focus of this solemn teaching. This sacrament is clearly not of the same rank and dignity as baptism or eucharist. However, the theological basis by which the various ritualized sacraments might be ranked as higher and lower has never been defined by church leadership.

2. Relationship to Christian spirituality. Illness is often a very difficult time of one's life. Feelings of anger, isolation and inadequacy are strong. A person is generally not as concerned about others, but too often very self-centered, because of the illness. Even in such difficult situations, however, God still loves us. When the emphasis for this sacrament is placed on the element "common" to all sacraments, namely, that in this sacrament we primarily celebrate God's action, then a major link to Christian spirituality can be developed. God is actively involved in our lives, even when we are sick, even when we feel because of the illness so focused on our own needs, even when we might wonder about the value of our human life. There are many sick people who feel abandoned by family and friends, but God never abandons us. In this sacrament we celebrate God's unending compassion, a compassion that cannot be "ended" by sickness and pain. Moreover, the celebration of the sacrament of anointing is meant to be a celebration of the entire church, *Christus totus.* Each Christian individually and each Christian community should be concerned to show care and love for those who are ill. This is not simply a hoped-for side-effect of the sacrament of anointing. All sacraments are primarily the celebration of the *Christus totus,* the entire community. The more individualized and privatized this sacrament is, the less sacramental it is. The more a church community is a healing community, the more sacramental this celebration of anointing will be.

2. THE SACRAMENT OF ANOINTING CONFERS GRACE

At the time of Trent, this effect was primarily understood as the forgiveness of sin. A secondary effect was the strengthening of one's love of God and love of neighbor. It cannot be said that the canons in Trent on extreme unction reflect precisely what is the solemn teaching—"defined" teaching on the effects of the sacrament. Rather, it is the issue that all sacraments confer grace which is the source why this solemn teaching of the church can be considered "defined."

COMMENTS

1. All sacraments give grace. The sacrament of the anointing of the sick is no exception. Grace is first of all God's loving presence to a human person. *Because* God is present, sin is removed. The opposite idea is theologically incorrect, namely: *because* sin is removed, God is present. This latter would make the removal of sin the cause of grace, and when this line of thought is taken, grace ceases to be grace. Gift ceases to be gift. Grace is a free gift of God, caused only by God's own absolute freedom. The removal of sin is caused by God's free gift of grace. God's free gift of grace is not caused by the removal of sin.

2. **Relationship to Christian spirituality.** The most intense relationship to Christian spirituality which this teaching of the church might have will be based on its connection to Jesus himself as the basic sacrament: Jesus was a healer. Healing is an essential part of Jesus' message. When a Christian comes to see the presence of Jesus as a healing presence, not a judging and condemnatory presence, but a presence of compassion and love, then one can find in the sacrament of anointing a true foundation for one's spiritual life. Jesus the healer, however, should be central to every Christian community, so that the Christian community itself is experienced as a healing community. Too often a church community is not experienced as a healing community, and as a result all the preaching and teaching about the greatness of the sacrament of anointing falls flat. A healing community, the church as a basic sacrament, will make the spiritual meaning of the sacrament of anointing ring true. In other words, the spirituality involved in this particular sacrament of anointing is based on and derives from the spirituality of the Christian community itself which celebrated this sacrament. The more a Christian community is experienced as a healing community, the more the gospel message of healing will be effective within the entire sacramental structure of Christian spirituality.

The Sacrament of Holy Anointing
Teachings of the Ordinary Magisterium

The major documents of the ordinary magisterium regarding this sacrament are the new ritual and the revised code of canon law. However, the single issue which the ordinary magisterium must face remains the relationship between the sacrament of anointing and the forgiveness of sin. Only when the ordinary magisterium of the church clarifies this issue will such documents as the new ritual and the revised code of canon law themselves become clear. In religious education, respect for both the new ritual and code will be present, but beneath this respect will be the hope that this major unresolved issue will be honestly faced by the hierarchical magisterium. Until this is done, religious education will continue to find both the code and the ritual documents which leave catechesis quite ambiguous. An honest discussion of this issue remains the single Unresolved Issue which still needs to be done. Almost every other unresolved issue connected to the sacrament of anointing is affected by the non-resolution of this single issue. Until this issue of the anointing of sin and the forgiveness of sin is resolved, no other major issue regarding this sacrament can be honestly faced.

8

The Sacrament of Holy Order

When a religious education teacher begins to prepare material on the sacrament of holy order, he or she sees immediately that issues regarding the institution and development of the church are so interrelated with the theological explanation of the sacrament of order that one must present church issues first, and only then the issues of the sacrament of order.

However, behind every presentation of the origin and development of the church, there are several competing ecclesial presuppositions; that is, there are different views regarding both the institution of the church and the institution of its ministry. These various competing presuppositions and views will affect the way a teacher presents a theology of the ordained ministry. Every selection of a particular approach and every set of presuppositions have definite advantages and disadvantages. This holds true when one studies the way in which Jesus instituted the church and its ministry. Teacher and student alike will read books by reputable Roman Catholic authors who have selected a specific historical approach and therefore a specific set of ecclesial presuppositions. Different authors, consequently, nuance the very same material or data on the institution of the church and its structures in quite different fashions. It is true that all views and all the underlying ecclesial presuppositions are fraught with many conjectures. No one particular set of these views or presuppositions enjoys any "immutable" veracity.

Every detailed presentation of the institution of the church and its ministry contains two different elements:

1. There are a *few* defined teachings of the church which constitute the "immutable" material in a presentation on the institution of the church and its ministry. One might call these the dogmatic

119

elements. These elements should be basically the same in every presentation of the institution of the church. Such elements are, however, very *few* in number.

2. There are the *many* historical details which are included in every presentation of the institution of the church and its ministry. These historical details are interpreted differently by different authors. These details can be called the historical elements of the presentation. Bishops and popes never "define" historical data; rather, they define religious truths. The *many* historical elements are therefore open to a variety of competing interpretations.

The way in which an author describes how Jesus established his church and how ordained ministry began will contain both the few dogmatic elements and the many historical elements. Each author's presentation will be evaluated with different standards: there is a *theological evaluation* on the way he or she uses the dogmatic elements; there will be an *historical evaluation* on the way he or she uses the historical elements. At times, a writer will claim dogmatic value for something merely historical; at times, another writer will claim historical value for something dogmatic. Whenever this happens, confusion becomes inevitable.

In the Roman Catholic Church, there has been a "traditional" way to describe the institution of the church and its ministry. From about A.D. 1900 onward, scholars have researched the historical background of the New Testament. This historical research has changed the way one views the "traditional" account of the church's institution. This research has indicated that many issues in the traditional account which were considered "dogmatic elements" must be considered "historical elements." This research has helped theologians focus more clearly on what is truly dogmatic and immutable and what is historical and changeable.

As a help to all the teachers involved in religious education, I offer the following list of the more basic "dogmatic elements" which are central to the institution of the church. In this list, I simply indicate those "problem-areas" which Roman Catholic scholars today are discussing in ways that differ from the "traditional" approach.

1. THE INSTITUTION OF THE CHURCH BY JESUS

It is increasingly more evident, both from historical data and from the hermeneutical methods used in biblical scholarship, that the gospels do not contain any explicit institution of the church by Jesus *during his lifetime.* The emergence of the Christian church is seen more and more as a post-resurrection event when the followers of Jesus, slowly and with difficulty, separated themselves from the many strands of Judaism. This happened during the seventy years after the resurrection. Slowly, the followers of Jesus became a self-identified religious group, which since that time has been called "church." This process took place *because of the Christ-event,* an event which includes in an essential way the life, the death, and the resurrection. Without the resurrection-event, a "church" as we know it is unthinkable. If one maintains that in the very lifetime of Jesus a church had already come into existence, it would be a church without the resurrection. The risen Lord, however, is central to the Christian church and is central to Christian faith. The institution of the church by Jesus, who lived, died and rose from the dead, is one of the major "dogmatic elements."

2. THE INSTITUTION OF SPECIFIC CHURCH MINISTRIES BY JESUS

If Jesus, during his lifetime, did not in any explicit way institute the church, then there was also no explicit institution of specific ministries for that church. *Jesus in his lifetime did not ordain bishops or priests.* He did not establish such ministers and give them any specific authority. The emergence of specific ministries took place after the resurrection. Once again, the impetus for the development of such ministries was *due to the Christ-event,* which includes the life, death and resurrection. In this sense, one can say that the emergence and development of such ministries took place under the guidance of the Holy Spirit and that these ministries were instituted by Christ. In this sense, one can say that ministry in the church is of divine origin. The divine origin of church ministry is clearly one of the major "dogmatic elements."

3. THE SPECIFIC NAMES FOR CHURCH MINISTRY: BISHOP AND PRIEST

Today, the accumulation of historical evidence makes it necessary to say that such names as bishop (*episkopos*) and priest (*presbyter*) were, at first, only two of many names used by the apostolic and sub-apostolic Christian communities for their leaders. The naming process did not reach a settled and generalized form until the end of the second century and the very beginning of the third century. In other words, it is only around A.D. 200 that one can say that a person with the title, bishop (*episkopos*), was considered by most Christian communities as the highest leader in that community and that a person with the title, priest (*presbyter*), was considered by most Christian communities as a minister of secondary rank. Because there were a variety of names for church leaders prior to A.D. 200, and because the two names, bishop and priest, were not consistently used as the standard names for church leaders, one cannot say: Christ gave certain powers to his apostles (the twelve) who then gave them to persons specifically called bishops (*episkopoi*). On the basis of the historical data of the first two centuries, this kind of statement becomes questionable. A teacher sees immediately that this kind of historical research raises fundamental questions about the "traditional" way of presenting the institution of the church. This historical research does not deny the presence of "dogmatic elements," but it does caution teachers and scholars not to turn "historical elements" into "dogmatic elements."

4. AN UNCHANGING DEFINITION OF BISHOP OR PRIEST

In the long history of the Christian church, the definition of a bishop and the definition of a priest have not remained constant. Over the centuries, there have been very substantial differences in the theological meaning of both bishop and priest. What we might call the "essential theological meaning of a bishop or priest" *today* might not have been the "essential theological meaning of a bishop or priest" at another period of our church's history.

As we have seen, the name "bishop" (*episkopos*) became the more common name for the main church leader of a local church only around A.D. 200. Gradually, these bishops developed ways of working collegially with other local bishops, and from A.D. 200 to A.D. 1000 numerous regional councils of local bishops were held. In these councils, both local and regional issues of church life and teaching were discussed and quite often settled in a collegial way. Bishops gradually came to be seen as a "college." From about A.D. 900 onward, however, a new element began to take place in the West, and only in the West. Local bishops who had previously been elected by the local church began to be appointed and confirmed by the pope, with little or no input by the local church. The local church community slowly lost their voice in the selection of their bishops. Because of this relationship to Rome on the part of local bishops, regional groups of bishops with their many councils began to diminish and more and more local and regional situations were settled by the pope. In this development, a bishop slowly came to be seen as a "deputy" or vicar of the pope. It was precisely this kind of bishop, with his relationship to Rome, that theologians and canonists of the Middle Ages defined. He was a minister who had a *dignity and office* within the body of Christ, the larger church. This dignity and office was not given to him by a sacrament, but by papal designation. Medieval theologians and canonists no longer described a bishop as part of the sacrament of holy order. When the long period of time from A.D. 1100 to Vatican II is considered in its totality, one has to say that episcopacy was not considered either by church leadership or by major theologians as a part of the sacrament of holy order. It is true that in our own century many theologians prior to Vatican II were advocating a different approach: namely, that bishops were a part of the sacrament of order. However, they presented this approach only as a "theological opinion." They had no statement of the hierarchical magisterium to fall back on. At the Second Vatican Council, the bishops adopted the approach of these theologians and officially stated that bishops were part of the sacrament of order and were the "fullness of priesthood." The bishops did not "define" this approach, and so it cannot be considered at this moment a teaching of the extraordinary magisterium. It is only part of the ordinary magisterium of the church; nonetheless, it is official conciliar teaching. Today, a priest becomes a bishop not by papal institution but by a sacramental rite. A new bishop is no longer "consecrated"; he is "ordained." In all of the above, one sees that the "essential theological meaning" of bishop has not been something constant in the teaching in the church.

The first extant ordination ritual which we know of dates from about A.D. 200. In this ritual, priests were ordained to provide counsel to the bishop. No mention is made that they were ordained to celebrate mass or forgive sins. In this ordination prayer, the role of counsellor to the bishop was seen as the main office of a priest. Gradually, because of pastoral needs, priests were allowed to be the main presiders at eucharist and, as time went on, they were allowed to be the main presiders at baptism, reconciliation, anointing of the sick, and much later in church history, at sacramental marriage. When this development of priestly ministry had occurred, roughly around A.D. 1100, medieval theologians and canonists began to present a theology of priesthood *based on the practice of priesthood in the Middle Ages,* namely: a priest is a person who has the power to consecrate bread and wine into the body and blood of Jesus and who has the power to forgive sins in the sacrament of reconciliation. This "theological understanding" of priest is called the "scholastic view of priesthood." It became the traditional theological view and dominated the theology of priesthood in the Roman Catholic Church from A.D. 1100 to Vatican II. At Vatican II, the bishops deliberately set the "scholastic view of priesthood" to one side and in its place described the theology of priesthood through the *tria munera,* or the threefold mission and ministry of Jesus himself: prophet, priest and king. An ordained priest is someone who shares in the teaching/preaching mission, the sanctifying mission and the spiritual leadership mission of Jesus himself. Since Vatican II, it is expressly stated in many official church documents, even documents from the Vatican, that the *primary mission of a priest* is to preach the word of God (prophet). Secondarily his mission is to sanctify (priest) and to lead (king).

As in the case of "bishop," we see that what the church today might call the "essential theological meaning of priesthood" may not have been the "essential theological meaning of priesthood" at an earlier time in church history. Because of all of this historical data, one must carefully distinguish the dogmatic elements (the immutable elements) from the historical elements (the changeable elements). Historical data raises questions about many details in the traditional presentation of the institution of church ministry.

None of these four points—and there are others which could be stated as well—make the task of religious education on the matter of the sacrament of order any easier.

Fortunately, there are a number of well-crafted books on the history of the priesthood which contemporary scholars have produced. However, even these books are not in total agreement with one another on all issues. Nonetheless, religious education teachers and students have at their disposal these various reference works, and the use of them will certainly enhance the way one understands the material on the sacrament of sacred order.

The Sacrament of Holy Order
Defined Teaching

1. HOLY ORDER IS A SACRAMENT AND IT CONFERS GRACE

This is found in the Council of Trent, *Doctrine on the Sacrament of Order*, cans. 1, 3, and 4, in which order is clearly called a sacrament instituted by Christ, and that the grace of the Holy Spirit is given to those ordained.

COMMENTS

1. That there exists a sacred ministry in the church is the core of this teaching. An important clarification was made by the revised code of canon law on this matter. In the former code, one reads that a clerical order was instituted by divine law. In the revised code, one reads that ministry is of divine law. The further specification of "lay and cleric" ministry is not of divine law. In other words, the terms, lay or cleric, are legal terms and typological terms, rather than essential terms. The same can be said as regards the term "order," a term which is not of divine law. Only gradually was the term "order" applied to Christian ministry, and the theological understanding of the term "order" has had, over the course of history, several diverse meanings. Some of these meanings have been more political and power-oriented, while other meanings have been less political and power-oriented.

2. Because of this backing away from "divine origin" for cleric/lay and order, one finds in official church writings today other terms, such as: servant-leadership, ministry, presiders. "Sacred order" is a term which is still technically used for this sacrament, but the term "sacred order," by itself, is not self-evident. It requires theological interpretation so that it conforms to the servant-ministry one finds in gospels. It is the servant-ministry of Jesus himself which gives theological meaning to the servant-ministry in the church.

3. That this ministry consists of bishops, priests and deacons is clearly the present structuring of ordained ministry within the Roman Catholic Church. However, as mentioned above, from about A.D. 1100 down to Vatican II, the predominant view of theologians and canonists was this: a presbyter, not a bishop, was the highest grade of the sacrament of order. The episcopacy was not even considered part of the sacrament of holy order. Only a few theologians during those 800 years argued against that position, but all in all from 1100 to Vatican II, the dominant and most commonly held theological and canonical position and the one which the leadership at Rome followed was this: the priest had the fullness of this sacrament. At Vatican II, for the first time since the high patristic period, the Western church reasserted that episcopacy was:

1. part of the sacrament of holy order; and
2. the bishop, not the priest, had the fullness of priesthood.

The statement that holy order includes three degrees: episcopacy, presbyterate and the diaconate, cannot be seen as "defined doctrine" of the church which has been "immutable." For too many centuries, episcopacy was deliberately excluded from the sacrament of order by theological presentation, by canon law, and by the ordinary magisterium of the church. The threefold division of ecclesial ministry into bishop, priest and deacon cannot be considered a "defined teaching" of the church, that is, a teaching based on divine law [iure divino]. In the course of church history, there have been too many substantial, official and theological changes on this matter.

4. As regards the diaconate, during that same period of time, A.D. 1100 to Vatican II, the majority of theologians would not have said that diaconate, though a part of holy order, was a "sacrament" of the church. As late as 1962, the majority of reputable Roman Catholic theologians, who compiled the best "manuals of theology," maintained that the statement: "diaconate is a sacrament," could only be called a "certain and common" theological teaching. That this statement could be called a "defined doctrine" was disputed by these theologians. Once again, the teaching that there is a threefold division of order into bishop, priest and deacon raises many unresolved issues, so that calling these three stages of order part of "defined Roman Catholic teaching" seems very doubtful.

5. Relationship to Christian spirituality. The ministry in the Christian church is only understood from the standpoint of faith. In other words, a bishop, priest or deacon must personally say: "I believe I am a bishop, priest or deacon." At times, the self-identity of clergy does not include or includes in only a small way this basic centering on faith. One says too easily: "I am a bishop." "I am a priest." Or: "That person is a bishop." "That person is a priest." If faith is absent, priesthood can never be related to Christian spirituality. One should say: "I believe you are my bishop." "I believe you are a priest." Or: "I believe I am a bishop." "I believe I am a priest." "I believe I am a deacon." When the roles of bishop, priest and deacon are experienced or considered more as sociological, political and structural roles, the relationship to spirituality diminishes. In these cases, the sacrament of holy order loses its full potential for holiness, for spiritual growth. When holiness and faith diminish, some clergy become "career" clergy. When holiness and faith diminish, some Christians consider their ministers more and more as "career" people. In both instances, one begins to lose sight of the fact that bishop, priest and deacon are sacraments of the one bishop, the one priest, the one deacon, Jesus. On the other hand, when one approaches the ministry of bishop, priest and deacon with faith, then and then only can these become a source of Christian spirituality.

2. THE BISHOP ALONE IS THE MINISTER OF THIS SACRAMENT

This is found in the Council of Trent, *Doctrine on the Sacrament of Order,* can. 7, in which one reads that bishops have the power to ordain and are therefore superior to priests.

COMMENTS

1. The above wording of this solemn teaching is somewhat brief. The *Catechism of the Catholic Church* makes an even more detailed statement:

Only validly ordained bishops in apostolic succession validly confer the three degrees of the sacrament of order [1576].

This way of wording can be found in many theological books on the sacrament of holy order, and at first reading one might not be too bothered by such a way of speaking. However, there is a problem with the use of the two terms: "bishop" and "ordination." At the beginning of the twentieth century, several instances of an ordination to priesthood administered by only a priest have come to light. These ordinations took place in the Middle Ages and were officially sanctioned by the papacy. As a result, some theologians have modified the statement on the power of bishops to ordain, stating that the bishop is the "ordinary minister" of ordination, leaving room for "extraordinary ministers," such as priests. These historical cases of priests ordaining men to priesthood with the approval of the Vatican have caused a great deal of theological argument. Some theologians even called such documents forgeries. Other theologians only admitted that priests, generally abbots, were allowed to administer the "minor orders," not the "major orders." Other theologians say that these documents allowed priests/abbots to ordain to priesthood. In all this historical turmoil, can one really say that the statement: "only bishops can ordain" is "defined"? It seems that the historical data requires some nuancing of this statement.

The word, "valid," also raises problems, since the Roman Catholic Church leadership has acknowledged and continues to acknowledge the sacramental validity of ordinations in the Eastern churches which are not united to Rome. Since they do not accept the papacy, are such Eastern bishops and the priests whom they ordain in apostolic succession? If so, then apostolic succession and acceptance of the papacy are two quite different issues. However, in other documents of the church, especially those which deal with current ecumenical issues, apostolic succession and papal authority are often considered two sides of the same coin.

Secondly, there is no clear evidence of any "ordination" prior to A.D. 200. Every description by scholars on the manner in which a Christian became a sacred minister within the church prior to A.D. 200 is at best conjectural. There are no clearly stated "ordinations" in the New Testament, and we actually have no clear indication of any such ritual in the apostolic and sub-apostolic church prior to A.D. 200. Technically speaking, it is difficult to use the term "ordination" with any certainty for data predating A.D. 200. Does "ordination" as such go back to the time of Jesus, the apostolic time or the time immediately after the apostles? The question arises: given the uncertainty of the way in which the earliest church communities selected and placed their ministers in office, can we call the ordination by a bishop, rightful as it is today, "defined doctrine?" Once again, we are confronted with the difference between the dogmatic elements and the historical elements. From the very beginning of the Jesus-community after the resurrection, there was a ministry. This is the dogmatic element. That this ministry was conferred only by a "bishop" and that the ritual was an "ordination" is part of the historical element.

2. It is, however, a matter of faith to say that in this sacrament, as in every sacrament, God's action is the primary action. The *calling* of a person to ministry in the church is God's call; the *commissioning* of a person to ministry in the church is God's commissioning. The liturgical actions are primarily celebrations of what God is doing, rather than a celebration of what we are doing or of what specific ministers might be doing. The core in every dogma or defined doctrine is not what a creature does, but what God is doing. In an ordination today, the bishop is a sacrament of God, a sign that God is calling a given person and commissioning a given person to be a minister within God's own church. For centuries, a bishop has been such a sign or sacrament, a perceptible sign of the action of God toward a given individual, and a perceptible sign for the local community, and, since he is bishop, for the church Catholic, the wider community. This is one of the reasons why episcopacy should be a part of the sacrament of order. Likewise, the one who is ordained is a sacrament of Jesus for the community. Every dogma or defined teaching never ends at a mere creature. The focal point of this teaching of the church is not on the "power" of the bishop, but on the more ultimate power of God, of which a bishop [or perhaps some other minister] is a sacrament.

3. **Relationship to Christian spirituality.** An ordination liturgy is a celebration in faith. In faith, we believe that God has called and is commissioning this person to be a servant-leader of the community. In faith, we believe that the bishop is a major sign or sacrament of this action of God for us. The bishop, as a sacramental minister, not only signifies in faith a servant-leadership for our own small Christian community, but the bishop is also a faith sign that God loves the whole church, of which our community is a small but integral part. In faith, then, we see in the ordaining bishop a sign or sacrament of God's loving action, of the church catholic, and of the unity within our own Christian community. In faith,

we also see in the ordaining bishop a sign that God is acting for us. As in every sacramental celebration, the spiritual depth can be found in those words of Peter: "Lord, I do believe. Help my unbelief." When we try to be men and women of deep faith, we realize that we have a humble faith: a humble faith that has a grace-filled strength as one struggles to believe and, at the same time, a humble faith that has a human fragility in our struggle to believe.

3. THE SACRAMENT OF ORDER CONFERS A CHARACTER

This can be found in the Council of Trent, *Decree on the Sacraments, sacraments in general,* can. 9, and the *Doctrine on the Sacrament of Order,* can. 4., which state that this sacrament confers a character.

COMMENTS

1. The same understanding of character which was mentioned for the baptismal character and the confirmation character applies here, and the same relationship to Christian spirituality as was mentioned above also applies here. The defined teaching of the church on sacramental character is twofold: (1) that a character is present in this sacrament is defined; what the character might be is not defined; (2) sacramental character is intrinsically related to the non-repetition of the sacrament.

2. Every further specification or explanation of the character of priestly ordination remains a theological opinion, nothing more. Even the relationship of priestly character to a priest's relationship to an ecclesial minister acting "in the person of Christ the head," [cf. *Catechism* 1548 and its references to several Vatican II documents] is a theological presentation, not a defined teaching of the church.

3. Relationship to Christian spirituality. The priestly character, just as the baptismal character, says something about God rather than about a human person. The belief in a sacramental character, with its basic connection to the permanence of the sacramental action of God, is a belief that God is ever-faithful. Neither the lack of faith nor the immoral behavior of an ordained minister will ever prevent Jesus from being the church's one and only true priest. When we say that we believe that the sacrament of holy order confers a character, we are really saying in faith: we believe that God will always give the grace of ministry to the church, that Jesus will always be the one true priest of the holy church.

The Sacrament of Holy Order
Teachings of the Ordinary Magisterium

There are many teachings of the ordinary magisterium on the sacrament of holy order. The rituals of ordination for deacon, for priest, and for bishop are primary documents for this ordinary magisterium. In these rituals the ordained person is described in spiritual and theological terms, which include many theological perspectives. Such theological perspectives are not defined doctrine. For instance, in the prayer of consecration for a deacon, there is a relationship made between the sons of Levi and the diaconate. There is a relationship made between the seven men mentioned in the Acts of the Apostles and the diaconate. Both of these relationships are theological opinions, not defined doctrine. Even though there has been a long-standing tradition in the Roman Catholic Church, relating the deacon to the sons of Levi and to the seven, there has never been any official statement to this effect by church leadership, and there is today an acceptable understanding of the seven which has no connection to the later emergence of deacons within the church.

In the prayer of consecration for a priest, the priesthood is connected to the seventy wise men who assisted Moses, to the sons of Aaron, to "companions of the apostles." Once again, these relationships are basically theological opinions, not defined doctrine.

In the prayer of consecration for a bishop, there is mention of a relationship to the apostles, and the bishop is called a "high priest." The relationship of bishops to the apostles is not all that clear in today's theology, nor is the use of a basically Jewish term, high priest, a defined issue of our faith.

In a subsequent ritual of ordination, these prayers will change and emphases will be different. For the moment, however, these rituals represent the ordinary magisterium of the church and must be honored as such.

In the revised code of canon law, another document of the ordinary magisterium, there are many issues which affect the sacrament of holy order. Regulations are made on the times for ordination and on the jurisdiction of ordaining bishops [cc. 1010–1023], on the requirements in candidates for ordination [1024–1032], on the prerequisites of ordination [1033–1039], on irregularities and impediments [1040–1049], on necessary documents, prescribed examinations, and licit registration of all ordinations [1050–1054]. Almost all of these regulations could be modified, changed, or in some cases removed. Nonetheless, these canons of the code are an official part of the ordinary magisterium of the church and must be respected and followed.

One could also cite the *Program for Priestly Formation,* which the bishops of the United States establish. This document is revised at regular intervals but is a mandatory and official part of the ordinary magisterium of the church. Various congregations of the Vatican also have issued statements which affect the sacrament of holy order; once more, they represent, in varying degrees, the ordinary magisterium of the church.

Since the sacrament of holy order is so intimately connected to the organization and structure of church leadership, any change in leadership structures and organizations will have some effect on the ways in which a deacon, priest or bishop must act. Many such structural changes took place after Vatican II, e.g., parish councils, financial councils, presbyteral councils, etc. These are all legitimate expressions of the ordinary magisterium of the church and must be followed and respected. None represent a defined situation in the church.

One other issue affects these documents of the ordinary magisterium of the church, and religious educators should be aware of this issue. The more closely and carefully the history of the early centuries of the church is developed, the more cautious one must be in the way one relates a later form of bishop, priest and deacon to the apostles, to the twelve, and to other ministries which one finds in the New Testament writings. The bishops at Vatican II were quite sensitive to this issue of historical data and both the document on the liturgy and the document on the church attempted, at least to some degree, to address this issue of historical verification. There has been a long-standing popular view on the way bishops, priests and deacons of a later period in church history related to the ministers and ministries of the New Testament. This long-standing view of ministerial history has buttressed theological presentations on the power and authority of church ministries. It often happens that a dispute over some issue of holy order is really a dispute over church authority. The issue no longer is sacramental but jurisdictional. The issue is no longer one of sacramental theology but of ecclesiology. Religious education teachers must be aware of this kind of transition.

The Sacrament of Holy Order
Unresolved Issues

It should not be surprising that there are many serious unresolved issues related to the sacrament of order. The changes made at Vatican II have intensified many of these unresolved issues.

1. THE RELATIONSHIP OF THE ORDAINED PRIESTHOOD TO THE PRIESTHOOD OF ALL BELIEVERS

The bishops at Vatican II stressed the priesthood of all believers, with its connection to the *tria munera* of Jesus. The bishops also stressed the ordained priesthood with its relationship to the *tria munera* of Jesus. After considerable discussion on this relationship, the bishops stated that there is an "essential" difference between the two priesthoods, but the bishops did not make any further elaboration on the meaning of this "essential" difference. The bishops left the resolution of this matter, which involved many theological issues, to subsequent theological discussion. This discussion is still going on and it has not yet reached any completion. As of right now, there are several different and competing theological views on this theme. Religious educators will find the issue somewhat unsettling as they attempt to unite all that Vatican II said about the *tria munera* (prophet, priest and king) to both the baptized/eucharistic Christian and to the ordained Christian. In their discussion, I would suggest that religious education teachers return again and again to the mission and ministry of Jesus and to the mission and ministry of the church itself. It is only here that one finds the basis for all discussion of the threefold ministry (*tria munera*), whether that of the priesthood of all believers or that of the ordained ministry.

2. THE COLLEGIALITY OF BISHOPS

Since bishops are the "fullness of priesthood," a theological understanding of episcopacy is necessary for an understanding of the sacrament of holy order. However, when one begins to discuss the meaning of bishop, the issue of collegiality immediately arises. Collegiality of bishops is a major unresolved issue. At the ordination of a bishop in the Roman Catholic Church, a bishop is *ipso facto* part of episcopal collegiality. There are not two rituals: one to become a bishop and another to become part of the episcopal college.

Several serious questions, however, arise: if those ordained bishops in the Eastern non-uniate churches are considered validly ordained bishops by the Roman Catholic Church, what is the theological reason why these bishops are not part of episcopal collegiality? We Roman Catholics consider them valid bishops, but not part of the college of bishops. How can this be if entry into the college of bishops occurs concomitantly with episcopal ordination? This is, to date, an unresolved, but ecumenically important issue.

Secondly, even though collegiality has become a frequently used term in the Roman Catholic Church since Vatican II, there are certain movements by some church leaders to restrict the notion of collegiality. For instance, regional conferences of bishops are not considered by some theological circles in the Vatican to be instances of episcopal collegiality. The theological reasons for the restriction are not conclusive. Regional councils of bishops for the first millennium of church history were the more normal way of governing the church and many decisions arising from these regional councils are considered even today in the highest esteem. Much work remains to be done on this matter of collegiality.

Thirdly, episcopal collegiality means all the bishops including the pope. It does not mean: *all the bishops except the pope.* On the other hand, the popes have been very defensive of their own independence. The relationship of papacy to episcopal collegiality remains one of the more difficult unresolved issues and the lack of any clear resolution appears in the struggles between national conferences and the Vatican curia; in the way in which the various synods of bishops have been regulated; and in the way several national bishops have been required to meet in Rome rather than in their own country.

3. THE RELATIONSHIP OF PRIESTHOOD TO CANONICAL CELIBACY OF THE CLERGY

In many official documents of the church, it has been said again and again that there is no essential relationship between priesthood and celibacy. Time and time again, Western church leadership has praised the married priesthood of the various Eastern churches. On a small but ever growing scale, married men are being ordained priests in the Roman Catholic Church. The canonical regulation for celibacy, however, remains the standard for Western priests. The justification for this regulation has become increasingly difficult. The more often that one states that the theology of priesthood is not essentially connected to mandatory celibacy—and there is no essential relationship—the more difficult it is to maintain that the "norm" of celibacy should be continued. The fundamental theological justification for celibacy of priests must be established on nonpriestly grounds. But this means that the two are essentially quite separate and separable situations. Serious questions continue to arise. When one adds to this theological and canonical issue the pressing pastoral need for more priests, the issue becomes even more complex. Why are so many Christians deprived of sacramental life because of a church regulation which is not essential to priesthood?

4. THE ORDINATION OF WOMEN

Even though there has been a *Declaration* from the Vatican which rejects the possibility of the ordination of women, the question of women's ordination will not disappear. There have been many documents of the official church in which the equality, dignity and freedom of every human person and every member of the people of God are stressed. These documents state unabashedly that there is not a different form of equality, dignity or freedom for men than there is for women. These two different ecclesiastical approaches: (1) women cannot be ordained; (2) men and women have the same equality, dignity and freedom, cannot help but clash.

Second, it has become increasingly clear from the history of the sacrament of order that women were ordained to the diaconate. More than likely, the role of the female-deacon was not identical to that of the male-deacon. Nonetheless, historical documentation attests that the woman was considered "ordained." The *Code of Justinian,* which was basically written by high-ranking clerics including bishops, places female-deacons in the order of clergy. If women have been ordained to deacon in the past, and the evidence for this is mounting, then the pressure to ordain women to priesthood also gains momentum. Religious educators will have no answers to this unresolved situation, and in the upper grades this can become a theme of volatile discussion. Once again, it must be realized that there is not a serenely perfect organic synthesis to our Roman Catholic Christian life. Issues arise and cause great turmoil. No one, not even the best of our church's leadership, has all the answers. No one is omni-competent. As in all things human, we struggle to remove inconsistencies and continually return to the primary sources of Christian life for guidance. In religious education classes, there are clear occasions when the better answer is this: the issue to date is unresolved.

5. THE ECUMENICAL ISSUES OF ORDAINED MINISTRY

In almost all of the ecumenical dialogues, there has been a serious discussion of ministry. Roman Catholic leadership does not recognize certain forms of ordained ministry within Protestant and Anglican churches. At times, Protestant churches do not recognize Roman Catholic forms of ordained ministry. Discussion of the reasons for this non-acceptance is fundamental. The majority of these reasons are ecclesiological in nature, not sacramental. In other words, the presuppositions and views alluded to above about the institution of church and church ministry come into play. These must be addressed first before ordained ministry as such can be addressed. In a religiously pluralistic society, such as we have in the United States, the personal relationships between Roman Catholics and Protestants will always be a factor. At times, this will lead to marriages, and then the pastoral and practical issues of "church" can become very acute. Until some further resolution of the divisions in the Christian church can be reached, these acute practical problems will remain.

As with every sacrament, there are certain unresolved issues of very serious consequence. Religious education will not have answers and solutions to any of these issues. On the other hand, good catechesis does not allow us to present any given material as though such unresolved issues either do not exist or are of no serious import. Religious educators, accordingly, will allow time for a discussion of the unresolved issues. In fact, by allowing for this kind of discussion, one is preparing a student for a better and more realistic way of living one's Christian life, since existentially we live both in an imperfect world and we live in an imperfect church.

9

The Sacrament of Holy Marriage

The *Catechism of the Catholic Church* begins with a description of the role of marriage within human life and the role of the sacrament of marriage within the Christian life [1601]. This is an important distinction for all religious education. Marriage is a part of all human life; the sacrament of marriage is a part of a Christian life.

Many theologians, who discuss the sacrament of marriage, begin their presentation with an overview of the Old and New Testament descriptions of marriage. When reading these overviews, a religious education teacher might want to separate the *religious truths* found in the material in Genesis on Adam and Eve from an overly simplistic approach to the *historical validity* of the Adam and Eve story. Students should realize that the religious truths do not depend on whether Adam and Eve really existed or not. Even though the Adam and Eve account might be mythological, there are still profound religious truths about the dignity of the human person, both male and female, about marriage, and about sexuality that the account clearly presents.

The New Testament material will deserve special attention by religious education teachers, but again there is need of caution. The presence of Jesus at the wedding in Cana should not be presented as an "institution of the sacrament of marriage." Neither the text nor the context exegetically allow this. Traditionally, however, many church writings have described Jesus' presence at Cana as the beginning of the sacrament, but today this scriptural interpretation would not be a solid position to take.

Jesus seems to have been unequivocally insistent on the indissolubility of marriage. Because of his reference to Genesis, to the very beginning of a union of a man and a woman, his insistence on indissolubility seems to apply to all marriages, not just Christian marriages. In the gospels, there is never a distinction between sacramental and non-sacramental marriages. On this issue of Jesus, preaching an absolute indissolubility, theologians and scripture scholars generally refer to Mark 10:1–12, especially verse 11:

> The husband who divorces his wife and marries another is guilty of adultery against her, and if a wife divorces her husband and marries another she is guilty of adultery too.

Romans 7:3 reiterates this approach to marriage:

> If she gives herself to another man while her husband is still alive, she is legally an adulteress, but after her husband is dead, her legal obligations come to an end and she can marry someone else without becoming an adulteress.

Jesus taught that all marriages should be a life-long, mutual commitment of husband and wife. In Matthew's gospel, however, this injunction for a life-long, mutual commitment is modified. In the two instances he speaks of marriage, he mentions that marriage should be life-long "except in the case of *porneia*" (Cf. Mt. 5:31–32; 19:1–12). Biblical scholars point out that there is some sort of "exception" made here. For two thousand years scholars have tried to unravel the exact meaning of the word *porneia* in this context and have arrived at no solid conclusion. Perhaps what one should note here is this: Matthew was well aware that Jesus had preached unequivocally that marriages should remain indissoluble. However, because of a pastoral issue called *porneia*—whatever this might mean— which was bothering the Christian community in which Matthew lived, some exception to the rule was being made. This kind of emphasis on a pastoral process of maintaining the ideal of Jesus' teaching but realizing that pastoral and practical life often lagged far behind any ideal can also be found in Paul. In 1 Cor. 7:10–16, Paul states that the message of the Lord is clearly for a life-long commitment in marriage (verses 10 and 11). But immediately he considers a pastoral issue and begins by saying: "The rest is from me, not from the Lord" (12). Paul goes on to speak of a difference in marriage because of religion: one party is Christian and the other is not. If the non-Christian party asks for a divorce, let that person have a divorce, is his advice. In open contrast to what Jesus said about life-long commitment, Paul permits divorce with its right to remarriage. Such is the conclusion of the best Roman Catholic biblical scholars today.

All of the above is the revealed word of God: *both* the unequivocal saying of Jesus on life-long commitment in marriage *and* the exceptions which both Matthew and Paul make. One cannot pick and choose. Rather, one must try to put all the elements together as best one can. It is evident to religious education teachers that there are many unresolved issues which surround the interpretation of these New Testament passages.

When one goes beyond the New Testament times, one sees that only gradually and over many centuries did church leadership get involved with the way Christians married. In the early centuries of church history, Christians followed the customs of their country as long as these were not in open conflict with Christian principles. Step-by-step, but in a very haphazard way, bishops began to assert church control over Christian marriage. As mentioned previously, marriage was not considered a sacrament until c. A.D. 1150. The reason why both theologians and canonists rejected marriage as a Christian sacrament was the issue of sexuality. How can sexuality, which more often than not involved some kind of sin, be a source of grace? This was only resolved when canonists and theologians made a distinction between the following two issues:

   a. the personal consent (the theological position) or formal contract (the canonical position) which is a sort of "covenant";

   b. day-to-day married life which included actual sexual relationships.

The consent or contract now became the perceptible sign through which God's grace could be given to the couple. This consent or contract could be considered a source of grace. The day-to-day married life, with its sexual involvement, was the living out of an initial holy contract/consent. As a result of this line of thinking, marriage between two baptized Christians, since A.D. 1150, has been officially considered by the Roman Catholic Church as a true sacrament of the church. When this occurred and only when this occurred can we speak of a sevenfold sacramental church.

Much more could be said about the history both of marriage itself and of the sacrament of marriage, but this would be a volume in its own right. Rather, let us turn to a listing of the defined teachings of the church regarding the sacrament of marriage, so that a religious education teacher will have a grasp of the basic "immutable" elements. Then, I will present the major issues from the ordinary magisterium of the church. This will be followed by a list of the major unresolved issues regarding the sacrament of marriage.

The Sacrament of Holy Marriage
Defined Teaching

1. MARRIAGE IS A SACRAMENT WHICH GIVES GRACE

This is found in the Council of Trent, *Doctrine on the Sacrament of Matrimony,* can. 1, which states that marriage is one of the seven sacraments and that it confers grace.

COMMENTS

1. Throughout its history, the Christian church, with a few ups and downs, has consistently upheld the goodness and sanctity of marriage. It is true that for a long period of this history, a celibate life was extolled above that of a married life. Nonetheless, even with this relativization of marriage, the Christian church has never taught that marriage was evil. Rather, it has consistently taught that marriage in itself is good and holy. This should be the starting point of any and all Christian presentation of marriage and of the sacrament of marriage in particular. Marriage, whether sacramental or non-sacramental, is a good and holy way of life.

2. Since sexuality is a central part of married life, sexuality shares in the goodness and holiness of a married way of life. At times the Roman Catholic Church has not consistently taught that sexuality was something holy and good. The view that the sexual life of men and women was vitiated because of original sin has too often tinged the church's teaching on sexuality. Sexuality may have been originally good, but because of original sin and concupiscence, sexual pleasure was too often portrayed as something evil, at least venially, even for married people. This negative approach can be found both in official church documents and in theological presentations. In spite of this past negativity on sexuality, there was a basic stance that sexuality comes from God and is blessed by God. This, too, should be part of the starting point for all discussion on marriage in general, on the sacrament of marriage, and on the meaning of sexuality.

3. Because of this deep-down positive evaluation of marriage and sexuality within marriage, Roman Catholic Church leadership, both theological and ecclesiastical, has generally reacted in a negative way to anything which seems to *trivialize* either marriage or sexuality. In many ways, this is the basis for the Roman Catholic opposition to such issues as divorce, sexual promiscuity both within marriage and without marriage, birth control, and abortion. As mentioned above, however, this deep-down positive evaluation of marriage and sexuality within the church has at times been overshadowed by a negative attitude.

4. The teaching of the Roman Catholic Church has been clearly stated in Trent: there are seven sacraments. Marriage is one of them. It is understood, however, that only those marriages which occur between two baptized persons are considered sacramental marriages; marriages between the unbaptized are indeed legitimate marriages, but they are not sacramental marriages. Religious education teachers must make this distinction quite clear, since almost all of the regulations of the church on marriage center on sacramental marriages.

5. Relationship to Christian spirituality. There is a deep spiritual depth both to marriage and to sexuality. Key to this depth is the aspect of love. The more that genuine love permeates marriage, the more spiritual it can become. The less marriage is permeated with genuine love, the weaker is the relationship to Christian spirituality. The depth of this love is, of course, God's own love. In the love of husband for wife, wife for husband, God's love is also present. God loves a couple when they are loving each other. God loves them when they sexually express their love for one another. In the love of each other, one experiences the love of God.

2. SACRAMENTAL MARRIAGE IS A MARRIAGE BETWEEN ONE MAN AND ONE WOMAN

This is found in the Council of Trent, *Doctrine on the Sacrament of Marriage,* can. 2, which says the marriage of Christians is a marriage between one man and one woman.

COMMENTS ·

1. Since one finds polygamy in the Old Testament, endorsed by divine favor (Gen. 21:12), Christian theologians have continually moved in a cautious way on this matter of the unity of marriage. Most often, theologians will say that polygamy is illicit among Christians due to a "positive divine law," namely, the New Testament statements cited above. The position of theologians is this: Jesus' statement on one husband and one wife in a life-long commitment constitutes this "positive divine law." This new law nullified the "positive divine law" of the Old Testament. Quite naturally, the question arises: if God by a positive divine law in the Old Testament allowed polygamy, is not polygamy *per se* acceptable? After all, God could not have allowed something which was intrinsically evil. The debate on this issue will continue to go on. All requests to the Vatican for an approval of polygamy made by missionaries in territories where polygamy is part of the culture have been rejected.

Nonetheless, the questions about the validity of polygamy continue to be discussed, since the theological view involving "positive divine law" has not been totally resolved.

2. Another, and possibly far more important, issue than polygamy is involved in this approach to marriage: namely, the commitment which a husband gives to his wife and a wife to her husband. There is little doubt that in today's world infidelity remains one of the most devastating causes for marital breakdown. The church's teaching on the unity of marriage clearly attempts to safeguard the sanctity of one's commitment to another. Religious education teachers should focus more on this issue of the sanctity of one's commitment in marriage rather than on the issue of polygamy.

3. **Relationship to Christian spirituality.** When a man and woman marry, they give a consent to each other that is very sacred. This consent should never be trivialized. Rather, the consent should be strengthened as much as possible during the marriage. In real life, marriage consent is often strong, leading to intimate times of love and devotion. At times, the relationship of husband to wife, wife to husband is strained. The church's concern for married couples should be most evident in these moments of tension. Even when the church's concern might not be evident, God's concern remains. God loves us when things go well and when things do not go well. This does not mean that there might not be occasion for separation and civil divorce. No one should live with another who violates the dignity, freedom and person of the other. In this teaching, the church is blessing the mutual dignity and freedom of one's person. Only in this mutual respect and love of one for the other is "unicity" of marriage a sacred reality. In so many ways, this "defined" teaching of the church is a tremendous affirmation of the dignity and freedom of each person. It is at this deep level of human life that one finds a strong relationship of this teaching to Christian spirituality.

3. CHRISTIAN MARRIAGE IS INDISSOLUBLE

This is found in the Council of Trent, *Doctrine on the Sacrament of Marriage,* can. 7, which upholds the indissolubility of sacramental marriage.

COMMENTS

1. In religious education today, a clear distinction should be made between an annulment of a marriage and thereby the allowing of a second marriage and a divorce, which does not allow a second marriage. In the

case of annulment, there is an official declaration that from the very beginning "no sacramental marriage" ever took place. Because there was no
sacrament of marriage, indissolubility plays no role. Something which
does not exist cannot be called indissoluble.

In the case of divorce and remarriage, the first sacramental marriage
is considered legitimate and valid, but it is now civilly finished or "dead."
Canonists and theologians, for the most part, maintain that a "bond" still
remains between husband and wife. It must also be recalled that church
authority acts on the basis that for two baptized Christians only a sacramental marriage is possible. In the position of the Roman church, they
cannot be married civilly. For them a civil marriage is no marriage at all.

2. It was mentioned above that the passages from Matthew and from
Paul seem to allow divorce and remarriage and that this interpretation of
these texts is upheld by the best of contemporary biblical scholarship.
Such an interpretation of the New Testament has caused considerable
discussion among theologians and church leadership. A religious education teacher, in all honesty, must admit that at the present time there is
considerable theological, canonical and biblical discussion on the matter
of an absolute regulation that all sacramental marriages must be considered indissoluble.

3. The Eastern churches do not "grant divorce." Couples divorce,
and from earliest times to the present the Eastern churches have realized
that mistakes are made, sins occur, people repent. A second marriage is
allowed to Christians in these Eastern churches, but the celebration of a
second marriage has no crowning. There is an aura of repentance about a
second marriage. This practice of the Eastern churches has never been
condemned by the Roman Catholic Church leadership. All of this raises
questions about the teaching of the Roman Catholic Church on the absolute indissolubility of sacramental marriage.

4. The statement from the Council of Trent, cited above, must also
be read with caution. Because of the fact that Eastern churches acknowledged in some instance divorce and remarriage, the bishops at Trent were
very careful in their wording of the marriage canons, so that they would
not condemn the practice of these Eastern churches. Accordingly, canon
7 cited above as also canons 3, 4, 5, and 6 state only some issues which
people at that time proposed as adequate reasons for divorce. These reasons for dissolving a marriage were all rejected by the bishops at Trent for
the Roman church.

5. **Relationship to Christian spirituality.** Given all of this, what can
a religious education teacher say to the class about the Roman Catholic
teaching on the indissolubility of marriage? That the Roman Catholic position is clearly one that defends an indissoluble bond is clear. That the

Roman Catholic theological position places the indissolubility of this bond in the commitment of husband to wife/wife to husband is also clear. The Eastern churches have a different theological explanation of the indissoluble bond, which allows these churches to acknowledge that a sacramental marriage commitment does cease to exist and that a second marriage is possible. In this we have two conflicting theologies and spiritualities. The Roman Catholic leadership will continue to maintain the indissolubility of sacramental marriage for another reason as well: namely, those who disagree with this position challenge the very authority of the Roman Catholic leadership to maintain its laws on indissolubility. Thus, we have not only a sacramental issue involved, but a challenge-to-authority issue involved as well. The relationship of this teaching of the church to Christian spirituality is not only a relationship to the sacrament of marriage but a relationship to the issue of church authority.

The Sacrament of Holy Marriage
Teachings of the Ordinary Magisterium

There are more teachings of the ordinary magisterium on the sacrament of marriage than on any other sacrament, since there are so many canonical regulations, explanations of canonical regulations, diocesan regulations, etc., on the sacrament of marriage. Not all of these regulations are of the same "official status" nor do they all have the same binding or authoritative quality. The revised ritual for the sacrament of marriage is also an instance of ordinary magisterium. Regulations for mixed marriages, marriages between Roman Catholics and Eastern Catholics, marriages between a Roman Catholic and a person who belongs to a non-Christian religion are all instances of the ordinary magisterium. Although all these instances of the ordinary magisterium are *per se* changeable, nonetheless they are official and must be honored as such.

The Sacrament of Holy Marriage
Unresolved Issues

There are very many unresolved issues regarding the sacrament of marriage. At the present time, the following issues are the ones which are the most pressing.

1. THE ENDS OF MARRIAGE

Because of the diverse response to *Humanae Vitae* and its regulation on birth control, there has been an enormous amount of discussion on the "ends of marriage." Basically the issue focuses on the role of sexuality in marriage: is its openness to new life central or is its affirmation and interpersonal support of the partner's love for one another central? This debate will continue. On most occasions, the focus of the argument is not on marriage or sexuality, but on the authority of church leadership. Can one disagree with this papal encyclical, even though it is not an infallible document? Some theologians have defended *Humanae Vitae* to such extent that they claim infallibility for this encyclical. Cardinal Lambruschini, who was appointed by Paul VI to address the press at the time when the encyclical was promulgated, made it very clear that this was not issued as an "infallible" document. Since that time, no pope has made a declaration that the encyclical's teaching is infallible. Theologians' views never make an issue infallible.

2. THE INDISSOLUBILITY OF SACRAMENTAL MARRIAGE

Mention has already been made of this issue, and some of the major reasons were also noted why there is theological debate over the matter. Since the issue of indissolubility is related to other issues such as the authority of church leadership and the meaning of human sexuality, to name only two, the discussion on this matter will only be resolved as these other issues are also resolved.

3. THE RELATIONSHIP OF SACRAMENTAL MARRIAGE TO A THEOLOGY OF HUMAN SEXUALITY

The entire issue of human sexuality is one which at this moment of church history is being radically studied. On this matter, church leadership will remain traditional, while various theologians and other scholars will take more ambitious positions. As mentioned above, the Roman Catholic Church has rather consistently reacted against any trivialization of sexuality. As a result, one expects church leadership to be more cautious and traditional during this reevaluation of the theology of human sexuality. From a sociological and anthropological standpoint, regulations on sexuality have almost always been much broader than regulations on marriage. This means that there generally was greater latitude for sexual activity, while more restrictions were placed on marriage. The reasons for this diversity seem to be focused on the maintaining of a given society. The church, too, is a society, and the regulations on marriage and on sexuality all have some bearing on the maintenance of the church as a society. All of this plays a role in the current theological discussion.

It is difficult to present an overview of Christian sacramental marriage which has no unresolved or controversial issues. There are, quite obviously, serious issues which have continued to cause theological problems as regards the theology of the sacrament of marriage. Religious education teachers will have to be very creative and allow much room for debate, discussion, differences of opinions, etc. In all of this, a good religious education teacher should be able to guide such discussion by pointing out those issues which are "immutable" and those issues which are "changeable." Teachers must again and again lead the discussion back to the spiritual depths of sacramental marriage and sexuality. To do this, they might once again relate the presentation of the sacrament of marriage to the four major issues common to all sacramental theology:

1. In the sacrament of marriage it is the action of God which is primary.
   What the couple does, what the priest does, is secondary. God is saying to the couple: I love you individually. I now love you as a couple. I am full of compassion and strength, and I will be with both of you in your day-to-day marriage.

2. Sacramental celebration primarily celebrates the paschal mystery of Jesus.
   The message of Jesus, his paschal mystery, is a message that the kingdom of God is at hand now. In married life, one will experience the presence of the kingdom. This is a kingdom of love, of mercy, of justice, and of unending compassion.

3. The Holy Spirit acts in the sacrament of marriage.
   One is never alone in a marriage. The Holy Spirit of God fills married life with holiness. The Spirit of God says: Look deep into your marriage and you will find in marriage itself, in sexuality itself, the holy presence of God.

4. The *Christus totus*, the entire church, celebrates a sacramental marriage.
   Sacramental marriage is the celebration of an entire community, and the host of this community is Jesus. It is Jesus who celebrates with each Christian couple and with the community surrounding them the height and depth, length and breadth of human love, which is a sacrament of God's own love. It is Jesus, the host, who blesses the marriage.

Selected Bibliography

Cook, Bernard, *Sacraments and Sacramentality,* Twenty-Third Publications.

Dallen, John, *The Reconciling Community,* Pueblo.

Duffy, Regis, et al., *Systematic Theology,* vol. 2, Fortress.

Hellwig, Monika, ed., *Message of the Sacraments* (8 volumes) Liturgical Press.

Lee, Bernard, ed., *Alternative Futures for Worship* (7 volumes) Liturgical Press.

Mackin, Theodore, *The Marital Sacrament,* Paulist Press.

Osborne, Kenan B., *Sacramental Theology,* Paulist Press; *The Sacraments of Christian Initiation,* Paulist Press; *Reconciliation and Justification,* Paulist Press; *Priesthood,* Paulist Press; *Ministry,* Paulist Press.

Vorgrimler, Herbert, *Sacramental Theology,* Liturgical Press.